Captive Congregation
My Fourteen Years in the Church of Bible Understanding

By James E. LaRue

Copyright © James E. LaRue
Cover design © James E. LaRue

All rights reserved. No part of this book may be reproduced in any form or by any electronic or mechanical means - except in the case of quotations embodied in articles or reviews - without written permission from its publisher.

First edition, June 2015
Second edition, December 2016

Table of Contents

Preface 5

Introduction 7

Chapter 1: A Walk in the Mall 9

Chapter 2: Moving In 15

Chapter 3: The Worcester Fellowship House........................27

Chapter 4: The Older Newly Saved House 41

Chapter 5: Closing the Jersey City House 53

Chapter 6: Spiritual Retards 63

Chapter 7: The Retard Program 73

Chapter 8: The Fall of the House of Woodland....................83

Chapter 9: Moving Back into the Cult 95

Chapter 10: I Will Work Harder..107

Chapter 11: Dreams 125

Chapter 12: The Criminal Element Takes Over 147

Chapter 13: The Kingdom of the Cults 169

Chapter 14: My Last Year in COBU....................................181

Chapter 15: Leaving COBU 187

Chapter 16: Free at Last...195

Epilogue 205

PREFACE

Everyone who was in the Church of Bible Understanding has a story.

This is my story.

Some people say that the Church of Bible Understanding is a destructive cult. Why is it a cult? And how, and to whom exactly, is it destructive?

I wrote this book to help answer these questions.

Introduction

During my first ten years in the Church of Bible Understanding (COBU), I believed in the claims of the organization and its leader and I accepted the reasons we were given for everything we were supposed to believe and do.

Groups like the Church of Bible Understanding have existed in the past. I learned this by studying Christian history, and more importantly, the history of Christianity in America when I was still in COBU. America has always been a fertile breeding ground for religion - for genuine religious movements, but also for the worst possible counterfeits and misrepresentations of Christianity in which the message of the Bible is twisted and people are manipulated by the leaders of these organizations.

Learning that the Church of Bible Understanding was not unique was one of the things that helped me to leave. All of the other strange groups I read about were cults. It was obvious. And I was amazed at the similarities between these groups and ours. We were just like them.

Over time, I realized that I needed to leave COBU and even that it was God's will for me to leave there. Before this, the idea that God wanted me to leave COBU would have been inconceivable. As far as the other church members were concerned, my decision to leave was evidence that I was losing my mind. It also meant that the devil was deceiving me and that I was in rebellion against God. Because how could God be showing me to leave God's true church? I tried to speak up about what was wrong in COBU and what was wrong with its leader, Stewart Traill, and about what God was showing me, but no one would consider anything I had to say.

But my main struggle was not with the other church members. It was a struggle to decide whether the devil was putting thoughts in my mind to deceive me or whether my perceptions were real. It was an intense struggle. And it took four years for me to reach a conclusion once I began to seriously question things. My blinders came off slowly as a result of long and painful experience and disillusionment. If these things hadn't happened to me, I might still be there, as many still are, giving up my life to serve the leader of one of the worst mind-control cults in modern times.

Chapter One

A Walk in the Mall

It happened one day in 1980 as I was walking through a mall in Worcester, Massachusetts. I had just left the library, where I was reading about world religions, trying to find answers about life. I didn't want to go home right away, so I decided to walk to the mall. I was carrying two books on Buddhism which I had checked out of the library.

Buddhism appealed to me because I thought it could help me transcend my problems. Maybe I could take a different viewpoint about my problems or rise above them. Some of the ideas in these books were hard to believe, like the time when the Buddha wanted to cross a river and he didn't have the fare to pay the boatman. When he saw a flock of geese flying overhead, he was inspired to use his supernatural powers to fly across the river like the geese and then he appeared on the other shore. Fine, I wasn't going to believe all of this, but there were some ideas in Buddhism that appealed to me, so I checked the books out of the library.

As I was walking in the mall, I was approached by a guy carrying a Bible who asked me, "Can I show you a verse in the Bible?" My first thought was, "Oh, no. A Jesus freak." I looked to my left and saw a stairway. I thought about bounding up the stairs and away to safety. But then I thought, "If he's into this, he must know a lot about it. I'm looking for answers. Maybe he can tell me a few things. I'll hear what he has to say." So I stayed to talk with him. He said his name was Chuck.

Chuck opened his Bible and began to show me verses and to explain what they meant. I thought this was great. We're having a discussion about religion. I showed him the books I was reading and started talking about Buddhism and about transcending my problems. However, Chuck's intention was not to have a religious discussion. Instead, he was doing what I would later come to know as "open Bible witnessing."

This seemed to go on for about 15 or 20 minutes. Chuck went from one Bible verse to another to make his points. Somewhere in the back of my mind, I had always believed the Bible was the word of God. Chuck pointed to a verse that said, "All have sinned and have fallen short of the glory of God." Somewhere inside of myself, I believed this. And here it was in print, in the Bible. How could I disagree with any of it? Maybe sin was the problem I was trying to "transcend."

It was no longer a nice conversation about religion, as Chuck continued to pursue his goal, which was to explain to me from the Bible that I was a sinner and that I needed to repent and give my life to God. By this point, I felt like I was hit by a hammer and from there on, it was a simple matter of Chuck leading me through the steps to salvation.

Chuck asked me if I was ready to pray and get saved. I said I wanted to go home and think about it. He showed me a verse that said, "Now is the acceptable time. Now is the day of salvation." Chuck said I had to pray and get saved right now. Because "now is the acceptable time."

When he showed me that, I decided yes, I wanted to pray and get saved. Chuck said we should walk a few paces to a fast food restaurant in the mall where we could sit and pray. As we were walking, there were teenage girls sitting on some benches who knew about Chuck and his activities in the mall. They took up the taunt saying, "Hey Chuck! You've got another one! Hey Chuck, you've got another one!" But by this time, I was convinced I needed to get saved and I didn't care that the girls were making fun of Chuck and by default, making fun of me too.

When we sat down, Chuck explained that he would give me the words to the Sinner's Prayer and that I should repeat the words after him. I had some last minute resistance. "Can't I come to your church later and do it there?" "No, you have to do it now," he said. I bowed my head and repeated the words he gave me. A strange thing happened. When we were done, I looked up, and everything seemed bright and happy and different. I had just gotten saved.

I'm sure this whole process sounds manipulative to some people. Those not familiar with cults usually don't realize that cult members believe they are helping people. As far as Chuck was concerned, it was not manipulation. He was telling me the truth and doing the best thing for me. He wasn't thinking about recruiting me so that I would defer all my life goals and give up fourteen years of my life to promote a cult leader's agenda and lifestyle. He wasn't intentionally recruiting me so that I would in turn, go out to recruit more workers under the pretense of offering salvation so they would move into the church and work in the church's businesses without pay, except for a small allowance.

I didn't know that this conversation had anything to do with joining a group, or how long I would be involved in that group. And I could not have known that I would leave The Church of Bible Understanding fourteen years later with just a few crates of books, a duffel bag of clothing and only a few hundred dollars in the bank, owning no possessions, property or investments and having never married or dated during that time. I had no family or children. I was glad to get out at age 36 and to have a chance to start over again.

I was later to come to understand the tremendous pressure Chuck was under. He and others were under constant pressure from the cult leader, Stewart Traill, who was known to members as "Brother Stewart," to go out and gather more people for the group. While at the same time, being under constant condemnation for their shortcomings as human beings and their lack of faithfulness to Jesus, or at least to the Jesus as portrayed by Brother Stewart. No one could be faithful enough, or if their performance was deemed acceptable for a time, no one could remain faithful long enough for Jesus to be satisfied with them. They would know when Jesus was satisfied with them when Brother Stewart said so. And, Brother Stewart was always telling them that Jesus was not satisfied with them.

This treatment had an unusual effect on people. It caused them to work harder. Much harder. In order to "please Jesus." In order to finally be found acceptable to him.

Initially, I was shielded from the negative aspects of "the fellowship" (as it was called) by my well-intentioned recruiters. I didn't know about all the people who had left the group. I didn't know what the criticisms by ex-members and by those outside of the group were. My recruiters put the best possible spin on everything. In fact, they believed this would help me, because I didn't need to know about the internal problems of the organization. I needed Jesus and I needed to grow in my faith as a new Christian. They gave me interesting Bible studies. They said that living in the fellowship was a wonderful way to live.

There was a bit of self-serving in all of this too. One of the things Brother Stewart was unhappy about was the dwindling number of church members, which meant fewer workers to carry out his plans. It was in church members' best interest then, in order to stave off some of that anger, to try to increase the size of the flock again with new members, fresh faces who were unfamiliar with the ways of fellowship life, who could receive "Christian training." And in rebuilding the fellowship to its former size (and income producing capability) maybe Jesus, or rather Brother Stewart, would be pleased with them once again. So, I was given the most gentle and sugar-coated as possible introduction to life in The Church of Bible Understanding. The way was paved with promises of joy and happiness, of purpose in life, of a bright future here and in the afterlife. The hope of being saved from a sinful world and of being saved from myself, a sinner. No, they said, I didn't have to move in and live communally with the group, but wouldn't that be the best way? That way I would always be surrounded by Christians in order to be strengthened in the struggle against sin, the world and the devil.

Chapter Two

Moving In

After I prayed with Chuck, I gave him my contact information. A day or two later, he called to invite me to the fellowship house on La Grange Street. It was a big old house in what used to be a nice neighborhood. There was an empty lot full of weeds and trash on one side. The house was not kept up very well and the rooms were filled with boxes and trash bags filled with clothes and other junk.

I started visiting regularly and I liked the "brothers" I met there. Chuck, who met me in the mall and who prayed with me to get saved, gave me Bible studies. I no longer felt strange about the whole thing. I felt happy. I met Gary, who I thought was really cool. And Rick. Most of these guys had long hair and beards. And they were all friendly and wanted to know how I was doing. I liked having friends. It reminded me of my college years and after a while of not having any friends after leaving school, it felt good to have friends again. The feeling of being among a group of peers which I first experienced with my friends in my college dorm meant a lot to me and this felt like that.

Why does someone join and move into a cult? Studies have been done on the subject and attempts have been made to identify the kind of person who joins a cult. The conclusion of one of the studies I read, not long before leaving the cult, was that aside from a tendency toward being idealistic, there is no typical cult member and that cult members come from healthy families, extremely dysfunctional families and everything in between.

My family was in between. However, the breakdown of our family structure and another attempt to go to college only to drop out and come home left me with an attitude to do anything, absolutely anything, to move away from home and to stay away, because I felt like a failure. From as early as I can remember, I was supposed to go to college and I had stopped going. I had no idea of what I wanted to do with my life.

I tried once more to live away from home, renting a room with a family I knew and taking courses at another college. I ran out of money by the end of the semester and I couldn't afford to live there and to keep my car anymore, so I had to go back home again. The next time, I went to school for three months in London and when I returned home, my father had left my mother, where they had been living in the new house they built in Florida. He was now back in New Jersey and had moved himself into the bungalow by the beach that my two younger brothers were renting. When I came back from London, my father said I could live there too. My brothers had rented this place to be their own pad and though they didn't talk to me about it, I knew they didn't like how my father and I had imposed ourselves on them.

On one of my long walks on the beach that winter, I remembered that Denise, an American girl from Worcester, Massachusetts I met in London, often talked about how she and another girl wanted to rent a two-family house in Worcester. She said that I could move there too and that they would live downstairs and that I could rent upstairs. I hadn't been interested in the idea at the time, but now, in my present circumstances the offer didn't sound so bad. I called Denise. Yes, they were still planning on renting the house. She invited me to come on up. They didn't have the house yet, she said, but I could live with her father for a couple of weeks until she got the whole thing together. Her father was separated from her mother and had his own apartment.

Her father, who was a doctor, was friendly to me. But by the third week, he said I should be looking for my own place because he thought this was only a temporary arrangement. And now, according to Denise, they were no longer planning to rent the house. And in the 20/20 vision of hindsight, it seems clear to me now that I was only used to make her boyfriend Doug jealous, because he was wavering in their relationship and not committed to taking it to the next level. My presence seems to have helped. I went out a few times with Denise and her brother and sister to the clubs where Doug was playing with his band and sat with them in the audience.

But now I needed to find a place to live. I got creative and I went to the local college campus where I thought I could easily find a room. There was a lot of off-campus housing available. I saw a notice on a bulletin board by two guys named Scott and Steve who were looking for a third roommate to share the bottom floor of a house and I called them.

When I met Scott and Steve, I told them I was a college student, but that this semester I wasn't taking any courses, but I would next semester. Scott and Steve were cool guys who were into sports and girls. Definitely not the crowd I was a part of in high school. But by having friends in college, I had learned to socialize and make friends and was able to pass myself off as an okay kind of guy.

I think this is the person I always was. I was outgoing and energetic as a little kid. But over the years, events at home and in school caused me to become a withdrawn loner who preferred to be alone and as a result, I was lacking in social skills. I regained some of those skills and that personality when I moved away and went to college, escaping my home environment where I was the least liked family member who often was considered worthless and even the cause for everything that had gone wrong with the family, or so I was told. I was also not a part of the high school scene because I was not accepted. That started in the third grade, when during a game of tag, it was discovered that I couldn't catch anybody, not even the girls. And it continued on during the rest of my time in school, where I was known as someone who wasn't good at sports. And even in high school, I still looked like a little kid. I looked about five years younger than all the other teenagers. All those factors pretty much assigned me to socially marginal status. I remember when a new girl moved to our school in the eleventh grade and in class before the teacher walked in, she was flirting with one of the guys by asking him the names of all the other guys sitting there. When she pointed to me and said, "What's his name and what's he like?" one of the guys said to her, "Don't worry about him, he's not one of the guys you want to know."

So, getting away from home and my hometown gave me a new lease on life where I could start over as an unknown and make some new friends in a place where I was not typecast as a loser. This is one of the reasons why I would move into the cult, if the cult were the only alternative to going back home.

I resisted the idea of moving in. I didn't want to. Other events and forces were to conspire to see that I did. As I said, the reason I was living in Worcester was that I wanted to move away from home. I resisted moving in because I still wanted my independence. But when my housemates Scott and Steve, the college students I was sharing the bottom floor of the house with, went home for the summer, I was going to have to pay the rent by myself and even though I had two part-time jobs, the rent was still too much. And when I went to see some rooms for rent, they also cost too much and when I tried to negotiate a better rent, no one would lower their prices.

At the same time, I was visiting the fellowship regularly and going out "witnessing" with the brothers and the offer to move in was still in effect. I should move in, they said, for my Christian growth because Jesus wants us to live in fellowship. Faced with the choice of having to go back home or moving in, I moved in. There wasn't much drawing power in returning to my hometown, where all I would have to look forward to was low-paying jobs and no friends. I made friends the first time I moved away and went to college and I was desperately trying to have that again. And now I had friends at the fellowship and it was either this or going back home and living in a rooming house, as my father suggested, and scraping money together for yet another attempt at college. After brief attempts at college in four different places, I wasn't willing to try it again, at least not from that base of operations. I still wanted to go to college, but maybe I could go to college in Worcester, and I was already living away from home now. I didn't want to go back home.

As far as voices warning me not to move in and having full knowledge of what I was getting into, I remember only one. There was a Christian from another church who called me when I was still living with Scott and Steve to tell me about his concerns about the group I was getting into. He suggested that I give it some thought. Maybe I could come over to his place and study the Bible too, he said.

But there was no comparison between this guy, whom I'll call Bob (I don't remember his name now) and the "brothers." I was with the brothers from the Church of Bible Understanding in the Worcester City Center. It was summer and hundreds of people were outside. The brothers were wearing their red "Get Smart Get Saved" buttons and walking up to people and handing out literature or approaching them with their open Bibles, saying, "Hey, can I show you a verse in the Bible?"

No matter how people replied, the brothers always had a ready answer. Sometimes it was humorous. Other times it was a dire warning about hell and future judgment. But the brothers were animated. And because of that, many people stopped to talk. The brothers, as far as I could tell, were "boldly proclaiming the message of salvation" and actively engaging people in real conversation about spiritual things. By copying what they were doing, I began to do it too and I found out that I enjoyed it. I believed I was doing good for people and that I was becoming an outgoing person rather than being quiet and withdrawn. I could walk up to anybody, no matter who they were, and say something to them and see them react to me. This was not a sense of power over people, but rather a sense of power over my former self and I became motivated and outgoing.

With the brothers, there was always something going on. Some people got angry and stormed away. Some people stayed to argue. Some opened up about themselves and their lives and these conversations were good. We were really reaching people and affecting them for the good.

By way of contrast, Bob and his sidekick were also there in the city center. They set up a little table and were also trying to reach people with the Gospel message. But they were timid and quietly handed out tracts and sometimes politely asked people if they would like to talk. No one stayed to talk to them. They didn't get anyone angry or upset, nor did they get anyone curious and interested. There were no hot debates going on over at their table. Finally, Bob and his friend resorted to a staged conversation, with his friend acting as if he were a person interested in the message of salvation and Bob acting as if he were witnessing to him. They spoke loud enough in hopes that passers-by would overhear them and in that way, get a piece of the Gospel message. "So," Bob's friend said, "did Jesus really die for my sins?" "Yes," Bob replied, a little too loud for normal conversation, "he died on the cross to take all your sins away." "And what," his friend said, "can I do to be saved?"

I thought this was pathetic. It was obvious to me who I was going to hang out with. With the COBU brothers, there were intense debates going on. And they weren't staged. Some people were angry and wanted to argue. Others were interested and wanted answers and they stayed to listen as we explained salvation from the Bible, perhaps in a way they had not heard before.

On the surface, the COBU message was the basic salvation message of historic Christianity. It was easy to explain once I knew it and it even had an effect on me as I explained it, because each time, it reinforced what I believed. But good things can be used for manipulative purposes and even though the rank and file members had no such intentions, the power structure of the Church of Bible Understanding had entirely non-biblical intentions of what to do with this message.

The message we were preaching itself was powerful and had an effect on people. Almost no one was neutral to it. As Jesus said, "He who is not for me is against me." Some people were offended by the message. The reason why this message can be offensive can vary from era to era. In our current era, one of the reasons some people are offended by the message is because it is exclusive. The Gospel says there is only one way to be saved and that if you don't believe in Jesus, you're lost. This doesn't sit well with the modern concept of diversity and pluralism. In earlier times, when exclusivity and the idea of "you're either in or out" was a given, the Gospel message was offensive to some people because it included the idea of forgiving one's enemies, which is an unthinkable concept in some cultures.

A curious thing happened when you talked to enough people. It became predictable what they would do. You could not predict what a particular person would do, but only statistically. For example, if you said to ten people passing by, "Did you know that Jesus died for your sins?" Two people would ignore you and keep walking, without answering. One would make a sarcastic remark. One would swear at you. Four would give a hey, wish I could talk, but I gotta get somewhere look. And two would stop and talk.

I know this commodifies people, in a manner of speaking. And it's hard for me to escape looking at people from this viewpoint even now sometimes. This was the first time I had experienced the commodity approach with people and it was like breaking the sound barrier and I was released from my former self, who had always been on the low end of the social pecking order and could only react to what people did, rather than initiating and causing things. I had always been so dependent and locked into what people said to me. I got whatever they decided to give me, and most of the time they didn't give me anything. And, because I was not very important and not noticed, I had little effect on people.

Sometimes when talking to people, I saw things about them, or made good guesses. A young man came up to us one time and I said, "Are you from Egypt?" He said yes. I said, "Are you 20 years old?" He said yes. Then I was going to say, "Is your name Mohammed?" but I hesitated. This was getting too freaky for me! So I said, "What's your name?" "Mohammed," he said.

Each time before I spoke, there had been a whisper in my ear about what to say to the young man. Was it the Holy Spirit showing me this about him? I have often wondered if I had not chickened out at the last moment, that with three accurate questions like that, the young man might have become a Christian because he would have felt that because I had asked with such knowledge about a perfect stranger, that the God I was representing was all-knowing and that this God knew him. Well, he looked Egyptian. He looked 20 and what is a popular name in Egypt? Good guesses on my part, maybe.

The responses that people gave, especially the wise guys, were so predictable. Each one thought they were so smart. The common objections were like out of a handbook. "What about the people in other parts of the world who have never heard about Jesus, are they going to hell too?" We said to them, "But you have heard the message, what are you going to do about it?"

This gave me a sense of purpose. And as Jesus said about our needs and wants in life, "Seek first the kingdom of God and his righteousness and all these things shall be yours as well." I was to learn that, at least in this case, it was not to be so. I thought that if I devoted my life to following Jesus, that he'd take care of all the rest. I thought that if we went out into the streets day and night, it would be an adventurous life and Jesus would take care of all the details. We might get locked up. Or shot. Who knows? The brothers talked about needing to be ready for a time of future persecution and that we needed to be strong and prepared. The brothers told me stories about the police (and angry parents) storming fellowship houses and locking up some of the church members.

One day, I was out witnessing with Rick and Gary and we got into a conversation with some teenagers. One of them said to Rick, "You look like Jesus!" It was a compliment. I had never noticed before. It was the hippy era, or the end of it, and a lot of guys had long hair and beards. Aside from the T-shirt and jeans, Rick would have been perfect for the leading role in a Jesus movie. The kid was right. Rick did look like Jesus. Amazing, I thought.

There was a cult in Worcester at this time and we often saw a band of people in white robes and sandals following behind a guy who looked just like Jesus. We said to one another, those guys are in a cult!

One day, when I came over to the fellowship house, Rick wasn't there anymore. He had left the church. Why people left was never explained to me in detail. People just disappeared, it seemed. This was to have an effect on me. Chuck, who met me at first, was also gone. I got a long letter from him, which I didn't fully understand, about how he had been sent to the Manhattan Training Center because he needed help and was not doing well with Jesus. I felt disappointed. Eddie, a brother from Haiti, not only disappeared but took a church van and the proceeds from a day of carpet cleaning when he left. Charles, a brother from Ghana, became "contentious." He had criticisms about the church and Stewart, and now he was gone. Gary didn't leave, but confessed to the brothers that he had been looking at himself in the mirror and thinking he was good looking and that he was fantasizing about "backsliding" and going back to the "world," so he could have a girlfriend again.

Through these events, I learned to be unstable and to lack trust in my relationship with Jesus. If this way was so wonderful, why were so many people leaving it? People seemed to be doing well and then suddenly, as if infected with some mysterious virus, they became estranged and left, some of them saying the worse things about the church. I was sheltered from the specific details and a spin was put on what these ones were doing. These people, I was told, became "contentious" (speaking badly about the fellowship and Stewart) because they loved their flesh and sin more than they loved Jesus, so they were telling lies about Brother Stewart as an excuse to go back to serving the devil and the world. It was at this time that I learned what a "backslider" was. It was a very despicable kind of person, whom evil had entered, like the way Satan entered Judas at the Last Supper. And backsliders almost always spoke negatively of Stewart and the church. (The word backslider was rarely used in COBU to describe a wayward sinner who needed to be compassionately brought back to the way.) I did not want to be an evil and wicked backslider. I would hang on at all costs and do whatever it took! I was afraid of becoming a backslider and losing my mind and my soul. I would apply myself to this way of life, and be good and faithful to it.

Chapter Three

The Worcester Fellowship House

So, now I had moved in and was living in the church. I soon left the jobs I had in a record store and a restaurant and began working with the brothers in Christian Brothers Carpet Cleaning, the church's carpet cleaning business. Around this time, I called my mother and told her I got saved. She told me that about the same time I got saved, she had gone to a crusade and came forward during the altar call to give her life to Christ. I thought that God saved the two worse members of our family at the same time, in different places. There is a verse in the Bible that says God chooses the foolish and weak things in the world to shame the wise and strong, and I thought we were proof of it. This would be a witness to the rest of our family, I thought, and I hoped that they would soon follow us in the footsteps of faith.

My mother and I had been at enmity since I was a kid. Now we were able to talk and we forgave one another and I apologized to her for the way I treated her when I was growing up. My mother probably didn't know much about cults, nor did anyone she went to for advice in her local church. They told her to keep in touch and that eventually I would leave and that talking to me about being in a cult might drive me further into it. (There is some truth to that advice. But people also ask me why my parents were not more forceful. One reason is that they didn't have anything for me to come back to. And at this time, I wasn't thinking of leaving.) My mother questioned me about how I got saved and she was satisfied that I was really saved and, as she said, that I was trusting in the finished work of Christ for my salvation. This is true. I had joined a

Christian cult, or as some people call it, an abusive church or a fringe church. There are different names for it, but it means a church with basic Christian beliefs, but with a highly manipulative arrangement.

Looking for esoteric beliefs as a way to label COBU as a cult was not an effective strategy for experts on cults. Most of the doctrine was quite normal, at least on paper. As they say, in principle, but not in practice. The most anyone ever seemed to state as evidence of Stewart Traill being a false teacher was that he denied the existence of the Trinity, which he did not. He just said that the word "trinity" was not in the Bible. And the man who had the "only true interpretation of the Bible," as he called it, said we had to speak only in Biblical terms. Now, Stewart's views on life and how people should live (such as living communally and giving up their lives in the world) mostly flew under the radar of scholars who wanted to refute him on Biblical grounds, because he taught basic fundamentalist Christianity. And as far as being a called false prophet by some, Stewart responded to that by simply saying "I never claimed to be a prophet, so how can I be a false one?"

But Stewart did have some unusual ideas on how people should live. One was that they had to separate completely from the world. (The Bible says to separate from the world and adds that the lust of the eyes, the lust of the flesh and the pride of life are of the world and are not of God and that we should avoid those things. But in COBU, "the world" meant "everything outside of COBU" and anything that competed with Stewart's influence and control over our lives). Family visits were discouraged, because our families were of the world and they would try to persuade us to give up following Christ or to take an easier way. I found out that family visits were discouraged when I talked to the brothers and sisters during

Christmas about wanting to visit my family. I was more open and forgiving toward my family now that I had gotten saved, but they told me that Christmas in the world is filled with deceit and that the meaning of Christmas has been lost to commercialism, which is true enough, but it shouldn't mean you can't see your family either. They said that if I went and if I didn't take a stand for the truth, I would be guilty of taking part in my family's denial of Jesus. Not only that, I would be selling them down the river by my acceptance of their denial. They said it would be hard for me to fight against the family script.

This was the first time I heard this reasoning and I didn't quite know what to do with it. There was a lot of truth to it, as far as the commercialization of Christmas and Jesus not being the real focus of the holiday, but the best lie is the partial telling of the truth, while leaving other important parts out. I would soon be subject to a lot more of this hocus pocus. Although it was the brothers and sisters who told me this, they all had learned it from Stewart.

I was soon to find out that this line of reasoning and these rules applied to all family events, including weddings and funerals. Stewart said that at funerals, people got together to lie to one another about how good the deceased had been and to say that the person was in heaven now, when really, they were in hell. And in order not to take part in this deceit, we would have to say this to our families if we went to family funerals. If not, we were taking part in their denial of the truth. For weddings, Stewart claimed that the couple was really just mating like two animals, because it was not a marriage based on Christ and therefore it was not a real marriage. And even worse, because the man was not basing his life on Christ, he couldn't stand up to a woman's manipulation, which meant the wife was controlling the husband. And even "Church

Christians" (Christians who were not in COBU), as Stewart called them, fell into these categories because without "the only true interpretation of the Bible," which only Stewart had and they didn't have, the closest they could get was some happy feelings about God, and other than that, they were deceived too. And they certainly did not have right marriages. Stewart said that without the true interpretation of the Bible, these men didn't know that their wives were in control of their relationships, so they were happy anyway, because ignorance is bliss. However, Stewart said we did have true understanding, so we couldn't be happy and dumb like the Church Christians and that's why we couldn't get married if we weren't completely faithful to the truth.

Stewart told the brothers that women were the enemy who would test us at every moment, to bring us down whenever possible. And why were they that way? It was their "Eve" nature, he said. Just as Eve tempted Adam to sin in the Garden of Eden, they would tempt us. After sin entered the world, God said to Eve, "Your desire shall be for your husband, and he shall rule over you," which meant that what had once been a pleasant relationship was now a power struggle, where the woman fought for control and the upper hand over the man, and in almost all cases, she had it, except for those true Christian men who had mastered true Bible interpretation and were therefore able to "rule over her," as Stewart ruled over his wife, Gayle.

According to Stewart, there was a method to the woman's madness regarding her desire for the man. Only if a man was able pass a woman's every test, could she trust in him and want to have a relationship with him, because then he was a true man. And it was hard to pass all of Eve's tests without getting "maneuvered" by her. If she ever did gain the upper hand over the man, she lost all respect for him. That meant he was not a true Christian man and she wouldn't want to have a relationship with a man like that, unless it was a manipulative relationship, with her as master and the man on a leash. But as Christians, Jesus was to be our Lord and this would be a great sin, in effect breaking the commandment, "Thou shalt have no other gods before me." And if the man passed all of Eve's tests, he had better not relax, because when he least expected it, she would test him again. It would be only over time, when the woman saw that all resistance was futile and that no trick worked on the man, that she would find, once she had given all that up, that she was free to accept the man's love for her and to just be herself.

In fact, Stewart told us that this was exactly what his wife Gayle did to him when they were first married. He said Gayle threw tantrums and locked herself in the bathroom during the initial stages of their relationship as she tested the limits of her power over him. Now she was quite content and sat quietly beside him at meetings and almost never said a word in public. I began to wonder why I would want to have a relationship with a woman who was continually trying to bring me down. I began to be defensive toward women, in an attempt not to be deceived by Eve, so that someday I also could have a relationship with a woman.

We came to believe that only Stewart was able to be what a man needed to be with women. Through the only true understanding of the Bible and having a clear conscience, he was able to overcome all women's tricks. (Stewart said that having no guilt by which he could be manipulated gave him the moral power to take a stand against women's evil.) Stewart was, if one accepted his teachings - and young and impressionable minds did - the only true man. He didn't directly say that about himself, but the conclusions were easy to draw. In order to be a true man, a man needed the light of understanding that came from the only true interpretation of the Bible, otherwise he was living in darkness and unable to do more than follow his animal desires and instincts. Men in the world were lost. And among Christians there were few, maybe none, who had a deep understanding of the Bible and were faithful to it. But Stewart had this knowledge and was faithful to it. So, he was a spiritual man, able to discern all things. We were only just beginning to learn true Bible interpretation, and as Stewart was always careful to point out, we were woefully lazy and unfaithful to what little we did know. The true and faithful Christian man had his wife, Gayle, completely under his thumb. And he was surrounded by young female helpers who were officially called the "Gayle Helpers." There were always about 20 young women living with Stewart. The official purpose of the Gayle Helpers was to help Gayle with her projects, but they likely did very little to help Gayle with anything. Gayle was not working on so many projects that she needed that many assistants.

Sometimes at meetings, Stewart provided us with demonstrations of his power over manipulative women who were trying to overthrow his plans. In one such meeting, in a session about church finances, he made it appear as if the women in the church office were trying to seize control of the church and that they had been quite successful at it. He was a master at feeding peoples' words back to them and altering their words in order to trap them into making confessions about having evil motives. Stewart made it appear that the women were confused about the system of record keeping by demonstrating to all of us that they didn't know what they were talking about. He pointed out that each one was telling a slightly different version of the story and that therefore they were all lying. He said that the reason they were lying was to hide what they were really up to.

This session went on for a long time, until the women were worn out from trying to explain that they were working in the best interests of the church and hadn't been trying to sabotage anything, which is what Stewart was accusing them of. For drama, Stewart bowed his head and said to all present, "It looks like they've got us." Then he revealed his Plan B. He gave a talk about manipulative women and how one must always have a Plan B, and even a Plan C ready, if necessary. This Plan B was an alternate method of keeping the records. There were essential pieces of information the women didn't have access to, which Stewart had controlled all along. He called this the "plug." Then Stewart told us a story about being in a rowboat with women. He said that when the man is rowing along on smooth waters, the women will always try to "pull the plug" to try to sink the boat as a way to create some drama in what was, until now, a smooth but boring life. His explanation was done with great humor and most of us were laughing. And how had Stewart been able to keep the women from pulling the plug when he was rowing the boat? Why, because Stewart was sitting on the plug, that's how! This brought peals of laughter from everyone, except for the women who were on the spot. The plug in this case was information that the women didn't have access to because Stewart hadn't left it in their hands and under their control, knowing ahead of time that they would "pull the plug" if they could. In fact, by having Plan B and sitting on the plug as he was rowing, Stewart had foreseen everything and had been in control all along!

Through such staged demonstrations, church members were warned about how they had better not try to get the best of Brother Stewart, because he was way ahead of us. Creating and then solving such fictional situations before our very eyes was one of his ways of demonstrating his great wisdom. We believed it was all true. We would also come to believe that Stewart was way ahead of each one of us and that he understood our deepest underlying motives for our actions and that he knew what we were "up to" even when we didn't understand it ourselves.

Stewart said that the women didn't even have to consciously intend to sabotage anything, but through carelessness, they had allowed the "wrong spirit" (the devil) to work through them. This also demonstrated to the young men that the sisters in the church had layer upon layer of hidden motivations which we would never be able to decipher or get a handle on or control, and that the sisters could easily manipulate us and we wouldn't even know it was happening to us. I gave up hope. It would take me years, I thought, to understand even the basics of this. This often caused the brothers in the church to be unkind and suspicious of the sisters, because of their fear of being overcome by them. This drove a wedge between the men and women in the church, and eventually this and other purposefully designed plans by Brother Stewart resulted in all relationships in the church coming to an end, except for those who left and got married. Some of those couples then came back, only to have their marriages broken down and ruined by Stewart in what passed for marriage counseling where he pitted the couple against one another, calling the woman manipulative and the man a pushover for not being able to contain and stop her behavior. This caused great frustration and often the couples broke up. For those of us who lived in and never left the church, there were simply to be no relationships or marriage. And any relationships that had begun, ended.

Stewart was often accused by outsiders of "forbidding marriage." According to the Bible, forbidding marriage is one of the signs of false teaching and is "a doctrine of demons." (This passage is in 1st Timothy, Chapter 4.) Stewart always stated that marriage was allowed and that marriage was a "byproduct of faithfulness to Jesus." And Stewart simply caused everyone to think it was impossible to be faithful to Jesus and continued to pit the men against the women with methods like those mentioned above. So, although Stewart did not officially forbid marriage, no one got close to marriage, or rarely even began a relationship after 1979. After that time, there were no more relationships or marriages and these conditions continue in the Church of Bible Understanding to this day.

Stewart's demonstrations of power over women were never openly about sex. He perfected the old patriarch look, long white beard included. He kept his philandering a secret. The women who know about it maintain a wall of silence. Maybe it's too painful to talk about, because that would also mean talking about anything they might have done, or what they knew about and remained silent about when it was happening.

Another one of Stewart's ideas was that we were not supposed to have our way. We were "spoiled American brats." He often used the story of the Israelites in the wilderness, who when they got tired of eating manna every day, complained to God about the menu. The Bible says God gave them what they wanted by raining quail down on them and then he slew them when the food was still in their mouths. So, according to Stewart, we could beg God for what we wanted or go after it, but even if God gave it to us, we'd be sorry. As usual, the truth was mixed with lies. If a person pushes hard enough for something they shouldn't have, God might give them over to it, after warning that person many times. But in COBU, this just meant that we could only do what Stewart wanted us to do. We had to live communally in cramped living conditions, although I came to the church after the time when brothers and sisters lived in warehouses and lofts in Manhattan with one bathroom for several hundred people, including children. They were washing in the public baths on Bleeker Street. That lifestyle ended because the city's board of health closed the lofts down. During that time, Stewart was living in his own house in Teaneck, New Jersey with his first wife, his children and a small staff of female helpers.

As with many things, in the Bible, it's all about the context. The context of the passage in the Bible about the manna was that the Israelites were rebellious and immoral and doing much more than complaining about food. It really wasn't about wanting something else than manna all the time. But we were a bunch of kids who maybe whined about lack of sleep or wanting some time off, but unlike the Israelites at that moment in history, we really wanted to serve God and Stewart was manipulating us by misusing the Bible on us like this. This was the real way in which COBU flew under the radar, as far as people wanting to label it as a cult by looking for odd doctrines. This was not necessarily apparent when anyone talked to a rank and file member and I wouldn't have called my parents to complain about this teaching or the practices it led to. Its effects were slow, like lead poisoning. COBU didn't kill you all at once. It was a slow death, a slow hardening of the arteries, as people became devoid of human emotion, harsh and condemning of one another and lived in denial of their basic humanity in the name of God. And to the degree it was their nature to do so, or to the degree they aspired to leadership positions, certain brothers imitated Stewart and pushed this way of life on the others. But to some degree, we all imitated Stewart's way of talking and thinking.

You may wonder why I didn't leave during this time. Many did. But I had been so shocked by what happened to me before coming to COBU that I considered this better than the last several years of my life. I often thought that God brought me low so he could save me. I also wasn't very independent and I didn't have good family connections to rely on. And, besides, the rank and file church members were friendly. The brothers I met in Worcester and those I met later when I moved to other places in the church were friendly and many were just like me. There was a critical mass of young people meeting together and it felt good to be a part of that. The only fly in the ointment, really, was Brother Stewart, but then again, he was the one around whom the whole church revolved and who we, to one degree or another, ended up serving in the name of serving God.

Stewart amassed a lot of wealth, but he was careful never to display it publicly. He wore simple clothing. He drove an old car with fading paint. He looked more like a handyman working out of his beat up old car than a rich televangelist. The whole COBU drama was played out in dirty warehouses, run-down residences and stacks of crates and boxes. It was an operation that thrived on the fringes of society, away from public scrutiny. It started as part of the Jesus People movement of the 1970s, as hippies living together in common houses. There were other people who lived in groups like this, but the times changed and they moved back into society. The Vietnam war had ended. There was little left to protest about and people were no longer dropping out of society, but rejoining it and moving on with their lives instead. The Church of Bible Understanding, originally called the Forever Family, was an exception that remained and continued to thrive on the margins of society.

It had originally been a loosely associated group of young people in Allentown, Pennsylvania who wanted to follow Jesus. Over a period of time, Stewart attached himself to the group. Because he was older than everyone else, he was seen as having great insight into the Bible and life. He gradually took control of the group. Where once church members had lived on an honor system, contributing to the rent and buying their own food, now everyone had to hand in their paychecks and receive a small allowance in return. Stewart sent people out to start new fellowship houses in many cities. Soon, he closed many of those houses down and moved church members into warehouses in New York City to be part of what he called the Manhattan Training Center. People who were there say it was to exert more control over the members and to mold them into a regimented income gathering force who worked day and night in the church's businesses. The fact that some ex-members now refer to this as the "Manhattan Draining Center" offers some insight into what it was actually like to live there.

I also learned that Stewart won every confrontation. I thought it was because God was on his side. One of the first confrontations I saw was during my first year, at a meeting for the entire church in Pennsylvania, what we called a Big Meeting. A group of ex-members disrupted one of the sessions and wanted to talk to everyone. One of them got into the center of the room, where Stewart was sitting in a chair. He grabbed the microphone from Stewart's hand and began to address the group. Stewart waited patiently to see how things would develop. He was using a tactic I would later come to understand better. He was waiting for his opponents to make one mistake. Stewart's entire way of life could be wrong, but if they made one mistake in their presentation, it would be all over. He would use it to the hilt. There were five men in this group of ex-members. There also was one woman, who after a while, could not control herself. She began to shout about how angry she was about being harassed and abused, working long hours and being subject to Stewart's humiliation of women. This was good, now there was an angry woman. According to Stewart, women were supposed to have a "gentle and quiet spirit." Stewart waited. The woman finally lost it and shouted, "I've had enough of this sh*t!"

That was it. It was all over. She swore. The men with her realized they had lost. I saw them wilt, as if all the strength had gone out of them. Until then, they had a pretty good discourse going on about what was wrong with the church and had succeeded in taking the floor, and maybe they were going to spill some of the beans about what Stewart was really doing. But now, because of this one word, they lost the battle for the hearts and minds of current COBU members. Swearing certainly meant that they were backsliders and this one word negated everything they said and any progress they might have made. Swearing was one of the things I gave up when I got saved, along with taking God's name in vain or even just saying "Wow, God!" whenever I wanted to emphasize something. One day, I was on the phone with Denise, who I've mentioned in this story, and I noticed that when she talked, she kept saying "God!" every couple of words. I had never noticed this before. Then I realized I had stopped doing this after I got saved, even though no one told me to stop. People in COBU didn't use God's name as an **exclamation point or for emphasis, and they didn't swear.**

The guy handed the microphone back to Stewart. In a show of compassion from the victor to the vanquished, Stewart said to us all, "Invite them to stay for the rest of the meeting! Talk to them, help them return to Jesus!" It was even more effective than saying, "Don't let the door hit you on the way out." I ran up to one of the guys and asked him to stay. He realized I was a naïve new church member and he said to me, "No, that's okay, I'm leaving." He looked disappointed. At that time, I had no idea of what these ex-members could have been talking about.

Chapter Four

The Older Newly Saved House

After living in the Worcester house for three months, it was time for me to move to the "Older Newly Saved House" in Jersey City. According to people who were in leadership positions in the church, this move was to rescue me from being ruined by the bad older brothers in Worcester so there could still be a chance for me not to become like them. Gary told me about this new house in Jersey City where "older" people like me, who had just gotten saved, could "be together with other people just like yourself to get training."

I was 23 years old, so I was considered to be older. I was not a "lamb," that is, I was not a teenager. The lambs lived in a church-owned property in Philadelphia called The Lamb House. The older newly saved were a special category and since enough older newly saveds had been coming into the church, a special program was created for us. I didn't want to leave Worcester, but wouldn't it be the best thing for me? Jesus wants you to, I was told. Stewart said that the older brothers were lazy and unfaithful and that if I stayed with them, I would become just as bad as they were. So, the older brothers in Worcester were giving up the only convert they had made in quite a while, because he needed to be saved from the very people who had helped him see the light, because they were setting a wrong example and could do nothing but ruin him.

Stewart pitted different groups of church members against one another to keep them focused their own shortcomings and on the shortcomings of others. Creating suspicion and distrust between church members was an effective way to divide and conquer, **to**

exercise absolute control over people and to keep them weak.

I was not happy to leave Worcester because I liked the brothers there, but I had already begun to be indoctrinated into the COBU worldview. I believed that the problems Stewart said I and others had were real and I believed what he said were the solutions to those problems. I didn't want to end up spiritually dead and on my way to hell, like the older brothers. I wanted life, so I decided to take the option that was being offered to me. I was soon on my way to Jersey City and to a memorable year in my life.

Sister Joanne was in charge of the Jersey City house. It was unusual for a woman to be leading in COBU. But Joanne was a personality and a half. She was older than we were, about 28 years old. The young women looked up to her. She was a role model. Everybody liked her, including the men. Joanne was all about Jesus. Jesus was her life, her everything.

Joanne was separated from her husband John, who according to Stewart, was one of the most evil people to have ever been in the fellowship. A backslider. As a new member of the church, it was never really clear to me what John had done wrong. Knowing what I know now, Stewart's efforts to break down personal relationships in general, and the marriage relationship in particular, was behind his character assassination of John. Stewart also targeted older brothers who spoke up about his own wrongdoing, portraying these brothers as backsliders and betrayers. His strikes against them were often vicious, and preemptive, if he caught wind that they had been speaking negatively (that is, truthfully) about him.

Stewart broke down relationships between us so that we would be loyal only to him and look only to him for guidance and direction. Under the pretense of marriage counseling, he broke up marriages by pitting the couples against one another. He discouraged any new relationships from starting and even discouraged friendships. We got come down on if we said anyone in the fellowship was our friend. Instead, we were "brothers and sisters" who were supposed to practice "loving one another," which more often than not, meant harsh criticism in the name of helping someone. This treatment of one another was not a good way to build close friendships.

Many of us believed John was evil. We had a lot of sympathy for Joanne, because she was a brave soul, soldiering on in spite of all her trials and tribulations. And the Older Newly Saved House in Jersey City was assigned to her. Although she didn't live there, she visited often. We liked her and she made our lives interesting.

Although at other times, she took so much control of everything that we referred to her as our "den mother." When we had to vote on something, whatever she wanted usually prevailed. This irritated us so much that one evening, when we were meeting together in the living room, someone passed a note around that said, "Whatever song Joanne votes on to sing next, everybody pick a different song so she doesn't get her way." Someone intercepted the note and handed it to Joanne. We waited to get come down on, but Joanne took it in good humor.

I was in this fellowship house from September 1980 to September 1981. Sometime around May, Joanne was pulled out by church leadership and replaced by Steve, an older brother with a whip to crack, who would not cut anyone a break. We were never told why Joanne had to go, other than that she was not doing well and that she needed further training elsewhere.

It was an end of an era. We used to go to downtown Jersey City to witness and lead people to Christ and then have Bible studies in the diner afterward, which Joanne called a "diner scene." We looked forward to getting together with Joanne at the end of the night, before she went back to Manhattan and we went back to our house in Jersey City.

At the diner, the sisters sat next to her and asked her questions. They all looked up to her for advice. She was one of the last good fellowship leaders in the church and an example of all that was right about the Church of Bible Understanding, before whatever was good about it disappeared. She was willing to be all there for anyone who needed it. She looked like she enjoyed what she was doing. If I were to say there was a best time for me in the fellowship, this would be it.

I'm saying this from the viewpoint of a new convert. I know now that anyone who was a leader was under tremendous pressure to perform and had to give account at leadership meetings. So Joanne probably had little enjoyment in what she was doing. No matter how well she did, it would never be good enough.

These were my early days in the fellowship, so I can only offer partial explanations and speculations about things. But it is good to tell the story this way, because it shows how naively trusting I was as a new church member. As time went on, there were no more illusions. But it was going to take me ten years to get to that place.

We often sang as we rode together in the van to go witnessing and when we were on our way to the diner. Twenty people crowded into a van, singing together. It was a really great time. There was a song called Wade in the Water, which was an old spiritual. There was a chorus to it that went,

"Wade in the water children, wade in the water. God's gonna trouble the water."

Then anybody could sing a verse, making up any words they wanted. One night, everyone was trying to outdo one another with their original verses. Mario, a brother from Ecuador, sang,

*"Tonight we're going to a diner scene,
Joanne's gonna tell us
what the Bible really mean."*

Then we all sang the chorus:

"Wade in the water children, wade in the water. God's gonna trouble the water."

These songs were a lot of fun to sing together. In just a few years, no one would be singing anything anymore. At this time, the church had not become what it would turn into in just a few years' time. I am not stretching it that far when I compare it to a death camp. I've read stories about prison camps. And I've met World War II veterans who had been prisoners of war. I could relate to what they were talking about. Unlike my situation, they couldn't walk through the gates of the prison camp to freedom if they didn't believe in this way of life anymore. But, until your mind is unlocked, it's as if there is barbed wire all around you and sentries keeping you in prison, and hardship and death if you try to escape.

We believed that leaving COBU meant immediate spiritual death and a miserable life in this world apart from Jesus, until we died and went to hell. When a brother protested to Stewart one time at a meeting that some brothers who recently left were not spiritually dead just because they left the church, as Stewart claimed they

45

were, Stewart countered with, "You're right, leaving the church doesn't make anyone spiritually dead. You backslid first and became spiritually dead, and *then* you left the church!"

Jim Jones told members of his cult that if they tried to escape into the jungle outside the fence at Jonestown that there were mercenaries out there who would shoot them. The scenarios that Stewart created in our minds were similar. No matter how bad and oppressive life was in the fellowship, life outside in the "world" seemed worse. And if we left, we were guaranteed to go to hell for eternity, because we were choosing to leave the only source of true wisdom and salvation. When we left, the forces in the world would immediately overcome us and pull us ever deeper into sin.

I believed this was true because this viewpoint was often reinforced by the testimonies of returning brothers and sisters who had left and gotten into sin, drugs, crime and worse. They came back to the church to try to rebuild their lives. Each one brought their horror stories of life on the outside. But what I didn't see were the hundreds who left and went on to have normal lives. These people didn't come back, so I didn't see examples of successful escapees. I only saw those who left and got into bad situations. They came back with their stories of how hard life was out there "without Jesus." The miserable sin-hardened faces of returning backsliders was enough to make me fear being swept away with the current of the world. Of all those who left, only a handful ever came back! These were the lucky ones. The rest were lost! This had a strong impression on me in my early days in the church. I would do anything not to be a backslider.

Around this time, I saw a strange phenomenon that I soon became familiar with. The strange behavior at meetings with Stewart. One day an older brother came over to the house in Jersey City and yelled at us, saying didn't we know the church was having a meeting at the YMCA? When some of us protested that it was a meeting for the older brothers and sisters, he kept insisting, so we went. When we got there, the meeting had been in progress for a while. Stewart was seated in a chair before the assembled older fellowship, several hundred in all, who were sitting on the gym floor without chairs. Soon Brother Stewart stopped speaking and all conversation slowly dwindled to nothing. Various brothers and sisters stood up to address everyone, a few comments came back, but soon, everyone was sitting in utter silence. Stewart was occupied with reading his Bible. He didn't look up or speak.

I began to feel an intense pressure. The force of everyone sitting in silence seemed to compel me to do the same. I decided to just read my Bible too, because if Stewart was doing it, it must be okay if I did it too. But this didn't help and I couldn't fight off the dense and choking feeling that settled in the room. This went on for at least an hour. The silence was overwhelming and quite literally, you could have heard a pin drop. Nobody was talking, nobody was moving. A man looked down at us from the jogging track that rings the upper floor of the gym. It was a strange sight indeed. This was not silent meditation or prayer. He stood looking down at us for a while and then shouted, "Hey!" And none of us moved or said anything. Then, "Hey! What are you all doing down there?" Silence.

The silence finally ended when Stewart looked up and began speaking. It was a long litany about what was wrong with the older brothers and sisters and their deplorable and depraved condition. He portrayed this in the most hopeless terms possible. I really had no idea what Stewart's purpose for using this technique was, or what was going on. Various ones stood up to offer their proposals on what could be done about it. They suggested plans and programs. They said they were going to repent and recommit their lives to Jesus. An older brother, Bobby, who was a bodybuilder, was speaking about recommitting his life to Jesus. I spoke up and told him that as part of his recommitment and getting more serious about Jesus that maybe he should give up the things of the world he was interested in, like his weights.

Now, this was the understanding about desires for things in this life that I came to have in COBU. For me it was the guitar. I felt guilty about playing the guitar now because my original reason for picking it up in college was to be like the guitar heroes in the rock music I listened to. Now that I was saved, I was no longer listening to "worldly music" as we called it, but when I saw brothers and sisters strumming guitars at meetings, I wanted to do that too. I couldn't **separate** out the original reason why I wanted to play the guitar, because it would be a temptation to play rock music, so for me, the guitar was an "idol" that I had to give up, even if others didn't have to.

I talked to an older brother named Harry who used to come over to Jersey City, to seek guidance on this struggle I was going through about wanting to play the guitar and about how some people told me I should stop. So I asked him, "What's wrong with playing the guitar?" He told me, "If you even have to ask that question, it means you already know it's wrong and that you have a guilty conscience." Such was the strange thinking in COBU. This thinking was certainly not a tool I could use to further myself in life and in the faith or to understand how to properly use my legitimate desires for the things of this world. There was a struggle going on inside me about playing the guitar, but that didn't necessarily mean that God and my conscience were telling me not to.

So, this was my first introduction to Stewart's methods, which included the silent meeting and other tactics. Later, I came to understand that before delivering his message to us, Stewart wanted to break us down first. That way, we were prepared for the message and it went in deeper. (His message was the next thing we heard after enduring this misery.) He did this by manipulating us to sit in silence for hours, feeling miserable, or by shooting holes in everything we said to show what liars we were, until we were worn out and gave up. After three or four hours of abject hopelessness, Stewart had now prepared us to receive his message, which was usually a long discourse about our hopeless condition. Then he gave us his plan for what we could do about it. This plan was the only possible solution to our problem and we were supposed to work at it.

When Stewart began speaking, many brothers and sisters opened their notebooks and began writing, trying to get every word down. Others had tape recorders. Though so many of Stewart's talks were taped, none of them were ever worthy of becoming a teaching series to be packaged and sold, like so many ministries do. They were often long talks about what God was going to do to us for being unfaithful to him. Or long Bible studies about the meaning of the symbol of the fig tree in end time prophecy, with supporting verses parsed into category and type. But, aside from some workbooks and pamphlets he wrote early on, Stewart never produced any materials to disseminate his message to the world, which seems odd for someone who claimed to have the "only true interpretation of the Bible," through a method he called "the figure system." Stewart claimed that God had given him "assured understanding." He also claimed that God had spoken to him and told him that he was going to use him to reach the entire world. If Stewart were entrusted with such a great commission to restore

49

the true understanding of the Bible to the world, it seems he would have been more forthcoming about it. But, with the exception of some tracts we passed out, COBU's teachings were for internal use only.

Stewart rarely taught on the life of Jesus or taught thematically through books of the Bible, where the meaning can be gained through the overall context of the book. He usually studied some small point in it, which he said was important, and it was often about Stewart's special understanding about the meaning of something, which he said no one else understood. He taught frequently on the second coming of Christ, but after a while, he refused to teach about it anymore, because he said we "just wanted it for entertainment." Brothers and sisters were enthusiastic about studying the second coming and came to meetings with Bible verses written out on stacks of file cards to read aloud and discuss. The verses were in categories like fig tree verses and second coming verses. This used to be very interesting. We stayed up late, sometimes doing an "all night second coming Bible study." It felt adventurous to be up late at night in a gym or a meeting room somewhere, studying the end times. It gave us a sense of urgency about it, that it could be in our lifetime and we were getting ready for it by studying the Bible and being able to read the signs of the times. As the Bible says, "From the fig tree learn its lesson: as soon as its branch becomes tender and puts forth its leaves, you know that summer is near. So also, when you see these things taking place, you know that he is near, at the very gates." (Mark 13:28-29 RSV)

Despite Stewart's hyperfocusing on certain issues in the Bible and centering his teaching around his claim to having the only true interpretation of the Bible, brothers and sisters read the Bible themselves and had a good understanding of it. The brothers and sisters seemed to have a strong faith in Jesus despite Stewart's treatment of them. Ironically, this faith is what kept many there. COBU's message was about a deeper calling and the idea of being sold out for Jesus appealed to many people. And brothers and sisters had their own experiences with Jesus and many had believed in him before coming to COBU. A brother named Jerry once told me that he had been working with another brother on a late night carpet job and they decided to take a break and pray. They both knelt on the carpet to pray and when they were done, they looked up at one another. Jerry hesitated to tell the brother what had happened, because he thought the brother wouldn't believe him. Then he told him that when he had finished praying and looked up at the brother's face, he had seen Jesus's face. The brother told Jerry, "I did too."

Chapter Five

Closing the Jersey City House

The older newly saved fellowship in Jersey City began its slow decline before I arrived, but when I moved there in the fall of 1980, there was still a lot of activity and the house was full. I was told that there used to be so many people living at the house or visiting that during meetings people were praying on the front and back steps because there wasn't room for everyone in the house.

When I moved there, there were about 15 young men and women living in the house, including two engaged couples, Fred and Donna, and Danny and Brenda. Relationships in the church were already on the way out. Fred and Donna told me they were surprised their relationship had survived, because so many couples had broken up (or had been broken up).

Danny and Brenda left first and not long afterward, Fred and Donna left. Both of these couples decided to stay together instead of following everyone else's example by ending their relationships and staying in the church. Couples who broke up and stayed endured the frustration of being able to see one another, maybe across the room at meetings, but not having anything else to do with one another. Some of these couples stayed on in hopes that things would change and that they could start their relationships again in the future.

After Joanne was removed from being in charge and Steve started coming to the Jersey City house, there were half the number of brothers and sisters living in the house as when I first arrived. This was part of an overall trend at this time, when nearly all of the older brothers and sisters left the church.

Steve was not the same as Joanne. He had an ax to grind and insofar as we could tell, it was because he wanted to get married to his fiancée. In the Church of Bible Understanding, the brothers couldn't just get married if they wanted to, they had to prove they were "taking the church by the hand" first. This meant that Jesus was number one in the brother's life, the church was second and his fiancée was third, and that he was a dynamic leader who was "out front" and "fully there" every moment of the day. Where did that leave the rank and file members who were not leading fellowship houses? Not only that, a brother had to prove his leadership ability to everyone and get voted on, and the atmosphere during any kind of voting was often adversarial, if not outright hostile.

This requirement for brothers to marry was in direct opposition to the Bible, which says in 1st Timothy, Chapter 3, that "If anyone sets his heart on being an overseer, he desires a noble task. Now the overseer must be above reproach, the husband of one wife, temperate, self-controlled...He must manage his own family well and see that his children obey him with proper respect. (If anyone does not know how to manage his own family, how can he take care of God's church?)" This means that a brother must prove himself to be an effective leader by being the leader of his own family first. There are different opinions on what level of leadership an overseer is, but the point seems clear that a brother does not have to be a leader in the church first in order to marry.

So, Steve was there to work on us and to work for a wife. Steve lacked Joanne's concern for people and was often rude toward any brother who was not outgoing or extroverted. He immediately went to work on me (and some others), saying that I was "weird" and "strange," and whatever other labels were handy in the COBU lexicon at the time. In one bullying session, Steve asked me in front of several others if I ever thought about hitting him. In COBU-style confessional honesty, I admitted that I indeed did have a thought about punching him, which occurred to me one time when I was angry at the way he was treating me (which I would never have tried, and besides, Steve was about twice my size). He turned this around on me to say how weird I was, because I had violent thoughts toward him, all the more proving what a weird person I was, just like he said. This was typical COBU bullying tactics and Steve had learned such ploys from the master himself, Stewart Traill. And as a result, it was acceptable for him to act this way toward people and no one was going to tell him not to.

Let me talk about some of Steve's motivations. I met Steve years later and he's not like this now. People caught in the web of the cults do all sorts of things in the name of wanting to do the right thing. And I would say that there are more good people in cults than there are bad ones and even the bad behavior is coming from good motivation directed at wrong goals or directed the wrong way at right goals.

Steve wanted to serve Jesus. And Steve wanted to get married. It was as simple as that. In many churches, that would have been no problem. In the Church of Bible Understanding, it was not so simple as that. Part and parcel of Steve's proving himself to be leader and worthy of marriage would be whipping those of us who were living in the Jersey City house back into shape. Steve wanted to serve Jesus and he wanted to "get married rightly," as it was called in COBU terminology. There was so much in that loaded statement, "married rightly."

People in cults are idealistic. They want to change the world for the better. The leader of the cult, who enjoys the financial rewards (and more) doesn't share these motivations. For cult leader, it's all business and what he can get out of this system he set up, and through which he controls people and finances. But the rank and file members are sincere people. That's why they work so hard. They believe in the stated goal of the cult, which is to bring positive change to the world. In the case of a Christianity-based cult like the Church of Bible Understanding, the stated goal is to bring salvation to the world. To save as many people as possible. To live in a community as an example of Christian faith and fellowship. To have relationships with one another based on truth and love – including proper marriage relationships. These were good principles, but in practice, it worked out so much differently for all those involved.

Although Steve was sent to whip those living in the Jersey City house back into shape, Fred and Donna could have done well enough as fellowship leaders. Until they left, they were the unofficial leaders there. And Joanne (and later Steve) were only around part time because they didn't live with us. So really, we didn't need another fellowship leader after Joanne was not coming there anymore.

I was disappointed when people left the church. Rich was the first person I met in Jersey City when I arrived. We sat and talked for a long time on the back steps of the house and we became good friends. He disappeared one day. After that Luchie left. Luchie (Lucien) and Bernie were two young men from Switzerland who came to America with no more plans than to live in youth hostels and to have a little adventure. They met the brothers and sisters and were treated so well that they moved in. Luchie went back to Switzerland and Bernie stayed in COBU for another 15 years.

Another good friend of mine, Brian, also left the Jersey City house. He wanted to leave the church and act in the theater. He was always torn between being in the church and being in the world. We had a lot of conversations about his struggle. When Brian decided to leave, I agreed to drive him and his few possessions to the apartment he was renting in Montclair, New Jersey. During most of the drive, I was trying to convince him to change his mind and to come back to the church. My friend Mario also left soon afterward.

I was now in the house with Victor, Linda and Miriam. Soon after, I helped Victor move to the Lower East Side to live with a relative. Linda went home to her family, and a few days later, Miriam moved to another fellowship house in Queens, New York.

I was now in the Jersey City house all by myself. Just nine months before the house had been filled with people. What followed were an interesting couple of weeks. I lived in the house and worked in the New Jersey branch of Christian Brothers Carpet Cleaners, the church's cleaning business, all by myself. I cleaned carpets during the day and sometimes went street witnessing by myself in Spanish areas in Union City, where I had a friend named Javier I was giving Bible lessons to. I also went to Manhattan in the evenings where I began to hang out with a group of older brothers who were separating themselves from the church. They seemed real and they were friendly. They were a kind of "cell" in the church who were living in a degree of freedom and at a distance from the usual oppression. They spoke a lot about God's grace and love and they never gave me a hard time.

When I was living alone in Jersey City, I started my workday by calling the answering service in the morning. Christian Brothers Carpet Cleaning had an advertisement in the yellow pages in North Jersey and there had been enough calls coming in to the answering service to keep Victor, Brian and me busy all day. Now I was alone. I called the people who had left messages and scheduled two or three jobs for the day. I went out with the van and the carpet cleaning machine by myself, cleaning carpets in the projects in Newark and in suburban towns along the New Jersey shore of the Hudson River. I worked hard and often drummed up a little extra business with the neighbors on the same hall in the housing project, cleaning someone's living room or entrance mats at a discount, because I was already in the building. There was a house in Union City where I came to clean a living room and bedroom but while there, I sold them on cleaning the basement stairs and their sofa and chairs. I spoke enthusiastically about the cleaning process and showed them how black the water was in the dirty water tank and convinced them they should get their other things cleaned too.

I dutifully handed in all the money to the church office.

I dialed the answering service one morning and there was no answer. I also got a call from someone in the Manhattan office who was yelling at me, saying that didn't I know that no one paid the bill for the answering service and that they had ended the account for the Jersey City house? I was getting come down on for being stupid and irresponsible, but really, I had no idea who paid the answering service. I never had that responsibility and no one passed it on to me when I was the last one in the Jersey City house. No one said they would pay the bill to reactivate the service again, nor did anyone seem to be aware of the income that I was bringing in as the only person working there. Maybe compared to the overall carpet cleaning income from all the teams working in Manhattan and the boroughs, no one had noticed, or maybe the income I was bringing in was so small by comparison that no one gave it a thought.

No problem, I thought, I'll just go and pass out flyers. The business had a little flyer with a drawing of a brother cleaning a rug and the words 39.95 Carpet Cleaning Special on it. I spent two weeks systematically leaving these flyers in the doorways of houses in a lot of towns. No one called in from the flyers. Apparently, the yellow page ads were the only advertisements that were effective in New Jersey and those calls had been handled by the answering service.

If the income from the work I had been doing previously had not been noticed, two weeks of no income was definitely noticed. Our friend Steve, who had previously been sent out to revive the Jersey City fellowship and who had not been around for a month, was once again called on the scene. Steve called and told me he had a job scheduled in a nearby hotel lobby and that I should go and join him to clean the rugs there. I walked in and heard a voice booming from the balcony above the lobby, "Come on, you lazy bum! Where have you been? Get to work!" It was hard to argue with the guy, because I did feel like a lazy bum after not working on any jobs for two weeks. Flyering could be counted as working, but there was nothing to show for it. And, if you've ever been unemployed even for a short period of time, you get a sinking feeling. I sure did feel like a lazy bum, although I didn't think it was right for Steve to treat me that way.

I was soon put out of the cleaning business. There were jobs now, though I'm not sure where they were coming from. Maybe the answering service had been reactivated and the work was coming from the phone book. Steve was now in charge and I was demoted to being his helper. I no longer had the feeling of accomplishment I had before. I was scrubbing the carpet with the wand and I wasn't fast enough for Steve, so he took over and made me just carry buckets of water. I was also supposed to anticipate where he was going to clean next and move furniture out of the way for him. I soon became bored out of my mind and I was standing next to the carpet cleaning machine in a daze. He saw that and came down on me for being a lazy bum who didn't want to work and he fired me.

Steve had been all about giving orders and insults. When I used to work with Victor and Brian, we talked to one another as we worked and I never got bored. I might not have been the fastest worker in the business, but we got the work done and no one thought it was necessary to report me for being lazy.

I wasn't the only recipient of Steve's cut and burn style of insulting people. When we finished work one day, we went to a restaurant and Steve decided that a woman in another booth was staring at him. In a booming voice, loud enough for the entire restaurant to hear, he said, "Don't stare at me!" She must have looked again, because he said, "Don't stare!" This was something Steve picked up from Brother Stewart. Stewart often abused people he said were staring at him during meetings. It was usually someone sitting in the front row watching him talk. One time, Stewart made a young man turn around and face the rest of the room, so he wouldn't keep "staring" at him.

I also was with Steve when we went into an auto supply store and he decided to berate someone behind the counter, but this time he was also talking about Jesus and the Bible while doing it. I walked out thinking, this is a horrible representation of being a Christian and what the Gospel is about.

After being fired, I took flyers again and went to Union City and West New York. After a couple of days, I got discouraged and lost motivation. I took a bus into Manhattan and walked into the nearest tall building, the McGraw Hill Building, and systematically knocked on office doors until I got a job as a data entry clerk in a health insurance company and I worked there for the next half year. I was bringing in far less money to the church in a week than I would have made in a single day when I was working in Christian Brothers Cleaning with Brian and Victor or those weeks when I was working alone, but no one seemed to care and no one bothered me about it.

Chapter Six

Spiritual Retards

When I was the last person remaining in the Jersey City fellowship house, I wondered if the house would be sold and if I would have to move to 515 West 47th Street, which was a five floor apartment building which the church owned in New York City's Hell's Kitchen neighborhood. In the 1980s, Hell's Kitchen still lived up to its name. I didn't want to live in this building because it was crowded and filthy. The rooms were packed with milk crates filled with literature, broken carpet cleaning equipment and trash bags filled with church members' clothing. People slept on foam mats on the floor. I didn't know anyone in the fellowship houses in the outlying boroughs of the city and I didn't know if anyone would allow me to live in one of those houses.

I felt temporary relief from wondering where I had to move when I found out that Jerry and his wife Pat (a married couple who didn't live in the church) were moving into the Jersey City house. When they announced that they were moving in, I said, "Great, and I can stay in the room on the second floor." Jerry said to me, "No, you don't get it. I bought the house from the church. You can't live here. It's our house now." I felt momentarily bewildered, because we lived communally and why couldn't I keep living there? (Married couples lived out and contributed a certain percentage of their income to the church, which was a wise financial move by Stewart to make sure the church didn't have to pay living expenses for couples and their children. Only the single people lived in. Single people had fewer attachments and were easily deployable to other locations at a moment's notice. They had no families to take care of, so they had no conflicting interests or legitimate enough sounding excuses to avoid the all day, and sometimes all evening and night, carpet cleaning work.)

Fortunately for me, I knew the brothers on West 46th Street in Manhattan, so I was able to move to one of the apartments there. I moved in with what little possessions I had, which included a wooden chair, a lamp and an Audubon print in a wood frame. Some brothers made fun of me for being "into house and home." I thought it was unreal. I didn't show up with a moving van, it was just these three things. The apartments on West 46th Street, which were rented and not in a building owned by the church, were much cleaner than the dump at 515 West 47th Street.

From September to December 1981, I lived in a kind of limbo. I worked as a data entry clerk in a health insurance company in the nearby McGraw Hill building on 42nd Street. I sat in a cubicle all day and entered medical claim information into a computer and talked to a Puerto Rican girl and a Brazilian girl who sat near me, mostly about silly things. By this time, I believed that "unsaved" people were as different from me as I was from them and that we had no topics of conversation in common, other than that I was supposed to witness to them, that is, to tell them about Jesus Christ and salvation, and that to become too familiar with them on any other basis would be inviting myself to be swept away with the current of the world, or at the very least, it would lead to "wrong agreements." Yet, I had to talk and be sociable, so I tried to make conversation.

In one of these conversations, we were talking about things like, if you had one wish, or if you had a million dollars, what would you do? We did this to pass the time and to alleviate the monotony of the boring and repetitive work. The Brazilian girl asked me, "If you could go back to any place in time and history, where would you go?" I said, "I would go back to the time when Jesus was on this earth and see him." It was the right thing for me to say. She said, "Come on really, where would you go?" I said, "I'd want to see Abraham Lincoln and visit some scenes in World War II," which was actually more what my "human" interests were.

I was also careful not to fraternize too closely with unsaved women, because this would certainly carry me into sin and make me a backslider. One time, we were all called over to the side of the room where our supervisor read an announcement to us. There was a young woman there who I often suspected was watching me from across the room. She came up and stood next to me and just once, gently tapped my foot with hers. I should have looked at her and said hello. Any comment would have been sufficient, but I kept staring straight ahead and acted as if nothing had happened.

Of course, I wasn't able to date or have a relationship with someone from outside if I lived in COBU. I would have to bring her over to the church and how would that go? Maybe if she got saved and moved into the church, something could happen, but what was the chance of that? Besides, there were a lot of nice sisters in the church who were Christians. Why should I look outside the church? At that time, I couldn't have known how absolute the ban on marriage was going to be. Brothers and sisters were married in COBU before, but there had been fewer and fewer marriages taking place until 1979, when the last couple got married. No one has married in COBU since. But at the time, who could have predicted the future and have known how it was going to be?

Our evenings were often occupied with going out witnessing, usually by doing "Art Shows." The Art Show was a series of 21 drawings on large placards, each showing a verse from the Gospel of John, Chapter 3, verses 1-21, which were used to explain the message of salvation. Twenty-one brothers and sisters stood in a row along the sidewalk, each holding one of the pictures while others went out to invite people to come and see the Art Show. There was another group of brothers and sisters standing at the end of the line of pictures who asked people if they were ready to pray and accept Jesus and be saved. Many did. The Art Show was an effective way to present the message of salvation. The drawings were done by a brother in the church named Bob, who was an excellent artist.

I knew enough Spanish to be able walk someone through the pictures in Spanish. I read each Bible verse that was on the placard and then explained it while pointing to the picture. There was a sister named Laurie who spoke Spanish and if she was in the line, she read her verse and explained it as I waited, and then I continued through the line with the person I was talking to. We usually went to Upper Manhattan, around West 181st Street or to Jersey City and Union City, New Jersey to do the Art Shows. When I saw the crowds of people coming through the line, I often thought that someday, we would be preaching the gospel around the world.

There were often periods when there was some program going on in the church, alternating with periods when a kind of benevolent anarchy reigned, when we didn't see Brother Stewart much, except occasionally at meetings. We ran things, made money in the church's businesses or handed in our paychecks if we had jobs in the world and went out at night and did Art Shows.

But after such periods, Stewart always came up with a new program to channel our efforts into a more focused goal. Most of the older church members (the long-term members, many of them there from the beginning) were leaving and there were a large number of what were called middle brothers and sisters just going through the motions, working and witnessing without any kind of control, program, lessons or reporting their activities to Stewart. So, Stewart came up with a program he called the Retard Program. I felt insulted by the name of this program and the reasons why Stewart said we needed it, but I soon found myself signing up for it anyway. Stewart said we were spiritually retarded because, although we had gotten saved, we had not grown in our faith and we were not properly trained as Christians. The implications of this were also that we would eventually end up in hell if we remained in this condition.

I heard that a group of middle brothers and sisters were meeting in 515 West 47th Street for the first Retard Program meetings, declaring their intentions to work at the program and proclaiming that they were spiritual retards and that they needed to be in the program. I thought, there is no way I'm going to join this. Though not openly, I scoffed at the program and at anyone willing to be in it. I read some of the materials, looked at the application form and felt insulted. (One of the things Stewart wrote on the application form was that since we were retards, we could fill out the form in pen, pencil – or even crayons if we wanted to.) But I also noticed that many of the sisters seemed to like this treatment, as if Stewart were gently teasing and playing with them.

One of the older brothers living at 46th Street said, "I was over at 515 last night and there were a lot of pretty middle sisters there." I was 23 years old and dating and relationships are extremely important at that age. I had also bought into the belief that I needed to marry one of the sisters in the church, along with the idea that (as Stewart taught) if I were not trained to be a Christian man, I couldn't get married. All of this was powerful incentive for me to change my mind about the Retard Program. (There were also a lot of pretty "young sheep sisters" and "lamb sisters," both of these being the younger and youngest age categories in the church, but they were off limits to me and there was no way I was going to be a church program where I could live in the same residence with them and maybe marry one of them. There were quite few young sheep sisters from the inner city I thought were very attractive and who had a certain way about them that I liked.)

Still, I had not joined the Retard Program. I began to take a hard look at the older church members and they didn't seem to be going anywhere in their lives or in their faith. (Which was not true, it only looked that way. Many were on their way to leaving and starting their lives over, outside the church. Their wiped out, dead and dull appearance was really the result of being overworked, tired and generally fatigued - and not from being backslidden and unfaithful to Jesus, which is what Stewart accused them of.)

My buddies, the small group of older brothers who had their own little fellowship group on West 46th Street, who listened to a preacher named Wayne Monbleau on the radio (and got made fun of for that and called "the Monbloids" by the others) and read verses to each another about God's love and grace, also began to be less of a source of inspiration to me, especially after I saw how they behaved at a Big Meeting. (A Big Meeting was when the entire church got together with Stewart for a weekend. These meetings were held at the Hamburg Fieldhouse in Pennsylvania at the time.) I drove with these brothers to the meeting and they were talking about starting a Christian band and writing their own songs, which sounded like a really great idea to me, and they were also encouraging one another with Bible verses about God's love. They seemed a little too worried, now that I look back on it.

When they got to the meeting, instead of acting like they believed that God loved them, and thereby being able to stand up to Brother Stewart's accusations about the older brothers' lack of faithfulness to Jesus, all of these brothers volunteered for guard duty as soon as we arrived and they remained in hiding for the entire two days. That disillusioned me. I thought we were all going sit together in the meeting.

I thought, maybe I should go for this Retard Program then. It seemed like the only hopeful way out. My alternatives were rotting away in "515" with the older brothers and never being able to get married. (But if I got trained in the Retard Program, maybe I could get married. I certainly could not get married without Christian training, I thought.) I could also learn how to evangelize and maybe preach Christ all over the world. I was interested in foreign languages and started learning Spanish after I got saved. And then I found out I could study more languages. (I never thought of learning more than one foreign language before. In high school, I chose one of the languages offered, and only one. So, I chose French, after agonizing that I wouldn't be able to study German, as if the two were mutually exclusive.) There were other brothers and sisters in the church who studied languages. A brother named Nathaniel was fluent in Italian. Deny said he wanted to learn seven languages so he could preach all over the world. COBU brothers and sisters really did want to "make Jesus known," as we called it. After moving in and becoming friends with Spanish speaking people who lived in the church, I got interested in Spanish language and culture. I had found my calling, or part of it, and I was looking forward to my future. Maybe I was going to preach the gospel to all nations – or at least to some of them. I was excited about going out to the Art Shows. When people got saved, I felt good. They also could come to know this way. The way of life in Jesus Christ, that is.

I didn't know yet that in the Church of Bible Understanding, I was expected to suppress all of my desires and interests in order to serve the organization and its leader. I didn't know I was expected to become a **cog in an** income producing and new convert recruiting machine, who was to receive nothing but a place to sleep and a fistful of dollars for allowance and enough to eat. (And plenty of coffee to stay awake. COBU was where I learned to drink coffee in industrial quantities.)

Really, I had no idea of what I was getting into or what was the true nature of the organization I had joined. I knew the people I lived with, those who were on the rank and file level, and they were sincere. I had no idea of the internal problems of the church, and of the reasons for the mass exodus of older brothers and sisters who were leaving the church. Older brothers could be "harsh" and older sisters could be controlling and **"maneuvering women,"** as Stewart liked to call them. There was something wrong with all of the older ones, according to Stewart. And, I would do anything not to become like them.

After resisting for a time, I filled out my application for the Retard Program. I saw no other hopeful avenue in the church, or for my life. Leaving the church didn't seem like an option. And I did not want to end up in hell.

I began going to the Retard Program meetings in Manhattan. Then we started having meetings at the Lamb House in Philadelphia (where Stewart was living at the time). I and several others were not backed in the voting to be in the Retard Program. I was 24 years old and considered to be older by the rest of those in the program, who were 20 to 22 years old, and so they said they didn't trust me, because I was "older." (Although I was not a very together person and I looked and acted much younger than I was. At one of the first

Big Meetings I went to, Stewart asked me a question and then added in a friendly tone of voice, "How old are you, lamb, sixteen?" I answered, feeling embarrassed, "No, twenty-three."

But I didn't fit neatly into any category in the church. I wasn't a young sheep (a teenager), and I wasn't an older brother (over 25). I came to the church at 23 as an older newly saved. There was still a chance I could be rescued and not turn out like the older brothers. I believed that the older brothers were as bad as Stewart said they were. I was deeply bought into the belief system of the Church of Bible Understanding, hook, line and sinker. I was completely caught and hooked. I believed in Jesus. I just didn't realize all the other stuff I had decided to believe along with that newly found faith. I was eventually to suffer the consequences, yet at the same time receive a life lesson that might be priceless.

So, I and a few sisters, who were really no different than anyone else there except that they were social misfits because they were introverted, were excluded in the voting at one meeting in Philadelphia. I felt disappointed about not making it into the Retard Program. But Stewart solved the issue with just a sentence, "How are these ones any different than the others?" And that was it, we were all in. I had been accepted into the Retard Program. My only hope against being swept away with the forces of sin in the world and being overtaken by the mysterious forces that seemed to make the older brothers and sisters weird and twisted mutants by the time they were 25 years old.

Chapter Seven

The Retard Program

I followed the forces that were on me and selected what I thought was the best option available to me. This caused me to get drawn more deeply into the Church of Bible Understanding. I decided to move to Philadelphia to continue in the Retard Program, because all other options seemed like dead ends.

I moved into the Lamb House in Philadelphia with about 80 middle brothers and sisters, ages 20 to 22. Most of them had been in the church for four or five years. Many of them were suspicious of me because I was "older," as if to say that the year or two that I had over them made me an utterly different kind of person than they were. (This was a dynamic that Stewart set in place. He goaded the younger church members to be suspicious of the older members. I was new to the church, so I wasn't an older brother, but I was still older than they were. The older brothers' fellowship had frequent meetings with Stewart, in which he always accused them of being unfaithful to Christ and said that they could do nothing right. The threat and the fear of turning into one of these older ones was useful stick for Stewart to prod the younger members of the church with.)

My other options had been to move in with the older brothers in the dirty and crowded apartment building which the church owned at 515 West 47th Street, or maybe to move to a fellowship house in the outlying borough of Queens. But when I visited the Queens house and put out feelers, I didn't feel welcomed there. There was really no other place to go, other than to follow the crowd into the Retard Program. In fact, when I considered the alternatives as they appeared to me, I felt fortunate to be included in the program.

All the middle brothers and sisters were now consolidated into this big house at 6713 Woodland Avenue, which was a former institution for the blind. There was a "brothers' wing" on one side with rooms for the men and the sisters lived in the "sisters' wing" on the other side. The two large living rooms and a kitchen, as well as a porch on the side of the house and a large yard, were common areas for everyone.

Stewart and his wife Gayle lived upstairs in this building but they never spent time with us and we rarely saw Stewart, except at some of the meetings. During our meetings in the main living room, we had to select ambassadors to go upstairs to talk to Stewart and to report on the progress of our meetings and to relay his messages back to us. These so-called ambassadors, more often than not, were sent back to us shamed and humiliated. A brother named Tim was the ambassador one evening and we sent him upstairs with our progress reports and messages. He acted intimidated in Stewart's presence, so he was sent back down to tell us that his new name was "Timothy Turtle," because when he was around Stewart, he went into his shell to hide like a turtle. Not only did Tim have to tell us his new name, but he had to explain why it was his new name. It was hard to find ambassadors, because after treatment like this, which happened all the time, most of us were reluctant to go upstairs to talk to Stewart. But, if we didn't send up ambassadors, Stewart accused us of hiding. He sometimes communicated these accusations directly over the little intercom mounted on the wall in the meeting room.

The lesson here was that we were supposed to be fully honest and fully "in the light" with Stewart at all times, without "hiding." Stewart said that he represented Jesus to us. (In the sense that he modeled Jesus to us by his "right behavior.") This bordered on the concept of Stewart being the only mediator between God and man, though he never said this. But then again, only Stewart had the "only true interpretation of the Bible" and without him, we were going to be deceived. If this was not directly stated, this is what it added up to, if we believed what he said about himself.

So, avoiding Stewart meant hiding from Jesus. One time when we were gathered together, Stewart asked us, "Do think you're in the light with Jesus if you're hiding from Stewart?" (He sometimes spoke of himself in the third person for greater effect.) A brother claimed that he avoided Stewart, but that he didn't avoid Jesus. Stewart countered with, "How can anyone say he loves God, whom he cannot see, if he does not love his brother whom he can see?" (This verse is 1 John 4:20: "For anyone who does not love his brother, whom he has seen, cannot love God, whom he has not seen.") So, with this bit of sophistry and misapplication and twisting of scripture, Stewart made himself the litmus test of whether anyone was with Jesus or not. A person had to prove their degree of faithfulness to Jesus by their connection to Stewart.

I just internalized these kinds of things. At 24 years old, and despite being in a Bible-based fellowship in which we read the Bible all the time, I lacked the critical thinking skills, life experience and the Bible knowledge needed to help me see through this deception - even if Stewart would have attacked anyone who stood their ground on this (or any) point, proving to them that they knew nothing. Or failing that, at least convincing all the others present what a liar the dissenting person was. In my early years in the church, I heard things like this and just believed it. And if I didn't believe it or had my doubts, my inward protesting against it was not enough to counter the all-pervasive kind of logic that Stewart used. Little by little, as I lived there over the years, I bought into these beliefs and internalized them, until they become a part of my life and my thinking. These were the unquestioned assumptions and rules that I, and everyone else there, lived by and interacted with one another according to. And layer by layer, I got woven into it, until it became my own worldview. And I lived with other people who also accepted this way and this reinforced it to an even greater degree.

Stewart's intimidating bearing toward people who were really just kids made it unlikely that anyone would be fully open, honest and trusting around him, unless perhaps you were a young woman he had decided to pursue and flatter with his attentions.

We were also supposed to go to Stewart for counseling. I did this once and appeared before Stewart, who was sitting at his desk in his office on the second floor. I came in and sat down in a chair in front of his desk and said, "Greetings in Jesus, Brother Stewart." He acted preoccupied and didn't look at me or acknowledge that I had entered the room. He was cutting photographic negatives with a pair of scissors, making a show of being busy. But one thing was certain, he was not going to acknowledge my presence as I sat before his desk. It was a game of intimidation, but as a young person before this great teacher, I assumed I was doing something wrong or that maybe I wasn't in a "right spirit." (That is, that I didn't have right motivations for wanting counseling and that therefore Stewart didn't want to "take part in my games.")

I sat in silence as Stewart carried on his act. I looked over to the other side of the room and saw Ann, a young woman he worked closely with to send out into neighborhoods to "gather young girls," sitting quietly at a small desk, writing. Once again, I broke the silence and said, "I came for counseling." Stewart remained silent. After waiting a while longer, I got up and said, "Well, I guess I'm going to leave now." When I got back downstairs, a brother named Tony was waiting with eager anticipation at the foot of the stairway (to get vicarious thrills from whatever happened between me and Stewart). He asked me, "So, how did your counseling with Brother Stewart go?" When I explained the bizarre scenario to him, Tony said it happened because I had been in a wrong spirit and that Stewart can see through my games. So, according to Tony, Stewart had been right to treat me that way.

(When I look back on this now and consider that Ann was in the room at the same time as my "counseling," the whole point of my treatment may have been that Stewart wanted to show Ann that all young men her age were hopeless idiots and that she needed someone older and wiser (such as himself) to be in a half-wife relationship with, rather than having a relationship with someone her age. So really, Stewart used character assassination toward me in order to magnify his position in her eyes. Ann was Stewart's "half-wife" - as he called such relationships - for a while. I didn't know this until I left the church many years later and read the stories Ann wrote about it, which she allowed ex-member Michael Montoya to publish on his website about the Church of Bible Understanding. When I was in COBU, all these things were kept secret.)

When we moved to the Lamb House (which Stewart had now renamed the Rescue Mission) in Philadelphia, we had to get jobs "in the world" because only a few brothers worked in the Christian Brothers carpet cleaning business in Philadelphia. Many of the new arrivals to Philadelphia, especially the sisters, were proactive and called ahead to arrange job interviews before arriving from the church houses in the other cities where they had been living. Some even had jobs already. Almost everyone else got jobs soon after arriving. I was one of the few who spent over a month job hunting. I finally got an ultimatum that I would be put out on the street in three days if I didn't get a job. So, I walked into a convenience store and got a job at the counter. I could have done that the first day I arrived, but I had been trying to get a "real" job where I could use my skills or feel I was learning something. Some brothers got jobs as dishwashers. I could have also done that early on.

Despite getting a job just in time, I was soon "outed" at a meeting by a brother who made the dramatic accusation that I was selling porno magazines at the counter of this store. This had become an issue for me because along with the sandwiches, coffee and cigarettes I sold over the counter, I was sometimes asked for this month's issue of Playboy, which was on a rack behind me. After selling a few issues, I began to feel guilty and I told the older guy I was working with that, as a Christian, I couldn't sell these magazines. After that, when someone asked, I stood back and allowed him to ring up the purchase instead.

I had also confided this struggle with my brothers at the church and that's how Steve O. knew about it and he soon accused me in a meeting in a dramatic way. "What do all the brothers think about Jim LaRue selling Playboy magazines?" There was a sudden uproar and I was now being dealt with in a confrontational style. There was no point in trying to explain the arrangement I had worked out with my coworker (who, by the way, reported this to the store management, which led to me being fired not long afterward). I was now being treated as an enemy of all righteousness and a wicked sinner and a criminal - and judgment was without mercy. The more I tried to explain, the more I appeared to them to be the very wicked person they were accusing me of being, because I didn't instantly lay down and calmly submit to this treatment. Because I became irritated at being pushed and shoved and accused without anyone listening to my side of the story, my irritation was now being used against me as evidence of me having an evil spirit.

In the middle of this, Jim G., who was considered to be second in command in the church, second only to Stewart Traill, popped his head into the doorway of the room and asked, "What's going on with this one?" Ah, I thought, Jimmy will help me. (I still believed in the integrity and fairness of the church's leadership and that they would judge with fairness and equity, and in this case, save me from the kangaroo court of the brothers' fellowship.) Someone answered that I was causing problems. None of the actual, objective issues at hand were mentioned and before I could begin to explain my case, I was shouted down by some of the brothers. Jim said that I looked like a troublemaker, because I was irritated and upset. He started labeling, a COBU technique learned from our leader Brother Stewart, who used it all the time. Jim described me to everyone as a dangerous conspirator and a promoter of strife, someone who is upsetting the order of things. I was sneaky and devious person with evil motives who had an honest looking face, the kind of face that could fool somebody, he said. Since my last name is LaRue, he mocked me by calling me "Lyndon LaRouche." (Lyndon LaRouche was a Marxist political activist.)

At this point, I began to undergo a change. It was same change I was to experience years later in a stronger form. As far as the standards of truth went, I saw that those in leadership roles who were supposed to exercise true discernment, fairness and judgment were willing to sell me down the river. I couldn't depend on such persons. But, I was not the biggest fish to be fried at the moment anyway. It was annoying, but the issue blew over. And besides, I was soon working at a job that a brother named Arnold recommended to me after the meeting was over. Until recently, Arnold had been working at an appliance repair store. He pulled me aside later and told me that if I went there and said I knew him, they would hire me, based on his own reputation as a good worker. I applied the next day and they hired me.

Jim G. has long since apologized to church members. Stewart used him to beat on us. He was Stewart's pawn, though I could not have realized this at the time.

The main activity at this time was our "retard training" which consisted of doing various rules (which we marked on charts with our names on them) and Bible studies. We also went out to neighborhoods in Philadelphia to gather "lambs," that is, we visited young people at their houses and brought them over to the Rescue Mission for lessons and meetings. Although the brothers and sisters worked together in groups, the relationships between them were usually awkward because the unreal life and teaching in COBU.

Stewart eventually brought out the awkwardness between the young men and women at one of our meetings. His punchline was, "All of his thoughts are, Jesus and sex don't mix." Stewart said that the brothers think that Jesus and sex don't mix and that they must choose one or the other, because they think they can't have both. And since they desire to serve Jesus, they choose Jesus only. Stewart said this in his usual dramatic way when a brother named Lou was standing up at a meeting and talking. Stewart asked everyone, "Why is Lou so uptight and unreal?" After a long build up to the point by making us guess the answer to his question, Stewart said that the reason why Lou acted so unreal was "because his every thought is that Jesus and sex don't mix."

So, now that the problem had been exposed, some of the brothers asked Stewart, "So what do we do?" But Stewart provided no answer, other than, "You must be proud of Jesus and proud of sex." The brothers kept asking, "But how do we do that?" But Stewart answered no further. This was the kind of advice we were receiving from this older person who was supposed to be our mentor and guide in all things spiritual and temporal. Maybe you can get some small glimpse from this scenario of the great havoc Stewart wrought upon our lives. I wonder if he did things like this just to embarrass everyone and make them uncomfortable.

I began to think I could never marry one of the sisters and that I should look outside of the church for a wife. I began to put my hope in meeting a young woman in the neighborhood where I went gathering and then she could become a "lamb" (a new convert) and move in to the church, and later I could marry her. There was a young woman named Adelaida (also known as Dolly) who I often went to see at her parent's house in North Philadelphia. Sometimes I went to see her with sisters from the church and sometimes I went to her house by myself.

Chapter Eight

The Fall of the House of Woodland

In June of 1982, I was still in COBU's "Rescue Mission" at 6713 Woodland Avenue in Philadelphia. This was the only time relationships between the men and women in the church started, and at least temporarily continued, during my entire 14 year stay in COBU. Although I never had a relationship with one of the sisters, I was the one who made the opening kickoff that led to Stewart declaring "Open Season," which was the beginning of a brief period when there were relationships again in the Church of Bible Understanding.

I knew about a teaching Stewart had for the Young Sheep Training Center, because I read the young sheep course notes and listened to tapes of the meetings Stewart had with them. The young sheep were newer members of the church who were in their late teens. Stewart had essentially cast off the older brothers and sisters (or acted like he did, because he still relied on their work in the church's businesses for income) and he was training these new young converts as the next wave of church membership.

As a middle brother at that time, I envied the young sheep because Stewart talked to them about being real people and about how they shouldn't be like the older brothers and sisters, who were so far gone and so beyond hope that their only purpose in the church was to be a warning to the new ones - and he said that the middle brothers and sisters were on their way to being like the older ones. "Doing your interests" (as well as "giving attention to the sisters") was part of the young sheep training. Besides working their day jobs and gathering new lambs in the evenings, Stewart said they were supposed to take time to develop themselves as whole persons by doing their interests, because this was part of Jesus's plan for their lives. I had never heard of anything like this, at least not in COBU. So I decided to do my interests and give attention to the sisters too, because I wanted to be a full and complete person, even though Stewart had never mentioned any of this as part of our middle brother and sister training. The young sheep brothers were allowed to show interest in the sisters by telling them "I'm attracted to you" and by giving them "attention." And, unlike us, they seemed to be on track for marriage, with Stewart's help. After receiving more training, of course.

I decided I would do what the young sheep brothers were doing and this is what precipitated Open Season at the Rescue Mission. When I was out visiting lambs with a sister named Judy, I told her I was attracted to her. After deliberating for a while as I was walking with her about whether it was right to do and what would happen to me if I did, I decided I was going to be brave and go ahead and do it. When I told her I was attracted to her, she had no idea of what to do and she freaked out. She was muttering to herself and acting nervously. It was an act of extreme damage control just to get her back to the Rescue Mission in one piece. Word got back to the brothers, who began giving me a hard time for breaking the unwritten rules and for "hurting" a sister. Some of them were using a phrase I had heard from time to time in COBU: "Are you trying to wolf away a sister?" There was no acceptable answer to this question, because it was really an accusation in the form of a question. The question was just shouted back at me again after I explained, or I got interrupted while explaining by someone shouting the question at me. All they could do is demonstrate a blind anger at what I had done.

A few days later, a middle brother named Ernie told me that Jim G. asked him, "So what do you think about Jim LaRue?" Knowing the issue and event being referred to, Ernie told me he was afraid and that he played it safe and replied, "Oh, I don't know..." and that Jim said, "He's just a brother trying to be real, in his own way." So then I knew that word had gone up to Someone Else's ears and had come back down and that I was not in trouble for **anything**.

And not long afterward, Stewart decided to call Open Season in order for us to get the unspoken attractions between us out of our systems. There were about 80 middle brothers and sisters living in this house, but relationships were a forbidden topic. Stewart said that the terms and conditions of Open Season were that any brother could tell any sister (and vice versa) that they were attracted to them, but that no one should take it seriously. He added that Open Season was to last for three days and that after having exposed all of our attractions for one another, we were supposed to forget about it and get back to business as usual. Despite Stewart's admonition not to take it seriously and to limit it to three days, relationships began springing up. Brothers and sisters began expressing their interest in one another and pairing up, with no intention of calling anything off, once those involved had decided that the attraction was mutual.

I was thrown out of the Rescue Mission two times. The first time, I was able to stay with some older brothers who lived out, but who were still members of the church, who owned a house at 4040 Walnut Street. Kevin and John, the owners of the house, regarded me with suspicion and contempt, and they often made fun of me. (No wonder I moved back into the Rescue Mission the first opportunity I got, where I had some friends.)

Moving back in was rather simple. When I was visiting my friend Steve B. at the Rescue Mission, Mike, a brother who had also been put out during one of our kangaroo court inquisitions, was let back in. I happened to be standing in the hallway when Mike was talking to some brothers and they gave him permission to move back in. I said, "If Mike is allowed to move back in based on that statement, that was the reason I was put out! I should be able to move back in then!" (Mike told the brothers that he didn't have any witnesses who could stand up for him to verify that he was faithful to Jesus, but that he would try his best. And, I had been put out for that reason, for not having "witnesses" to "back me," even though I said I was committed to trying.) Brother Roger (an old, spiritual man who was living with us) asked the brothers what was so different between me and Mike that he would be let back in and I wouldn't. So the brothers let me back in.

The second time I got put out, the circumstances were different. I was allowed to make one phone call before I was put out the door of the Rescue Mission around midnight, so I called Kevin and John and they told me they would let me stay at their house for only one night. I didn't know where I was going to sleep the next night. But I remembered how I found a room once before in Worcester just before meeting the church, so I walked to a nearby university to look for off-campus housing and I found a rooming house.

This time, the issue was that I had not handed in my paychecks to the brother who handled the money and allowances. Whenever he asked me to hand in my paycheck from my job at the appliance repair shop where I worked, I always said, "Sure, I'll get it to you later." For some reason, I was reluctant to walk to my room and get it for him at that moment.

Because I didn't get around to handing in two checks, he didn't give me my allowance, so I cashed my next paycheck so I could have money to buy lunch. This led to a confrontation at a meeting and I was able to keep everyone at bay for a while. I handled all their questions about whether I was saving up money to leave the church, or if I was guilty of the sin of the love of money, explaining that none of this was true. I said I still had the checks in my room, and that because I had not received my allowance, I cashed my most recent paycheck for lunch money. They asked me to get the checks, so I went to my room and brought the checks back into the meeting. But by this time, everyone was in a rage and they wouldn't let me sit down or leave me alone.

At that time, Jim G. walked into the room. I had a sense of relief (again), thinking he might help me. But Jim asked, "What's this one doing?" (I didn't have a name, I guess. I should have realized from his opening comment what was about to go down.) If I had been Mitch or Frank or someone, Jim might have called me by name and asked, "Hey, what's up? What have you been doing?" Such things would often happen. The brother or sister got talked to, the issues got dealt with. It might even be embarrassing for them, like the time Frank was saying he was attracted to a sister and they wouldn't let him sit down until he said who it was. But that didn't lead to him being put out on the street just minutes later.

After hearing various ones' explanations about what I was "up to," Jim asked everyone, "So what should we do with him then?" A lot of the brothers began standing up and making angry gestures and shouting that I should be put out immediately. If there were others who didn't agree, and I don't know if there were, they wouldn't have been heard anyway over the sound of the uproar and the anger that was being directed at me.

I asked if I could make a phone call first and four of the strongest brothers in the house escorted me to the phone room. I noticed that all four of these brothers were afraid of me. But, for some reason, I was surprisingly calm during this whole episode. I even found it humorous that they were afraid of me, because there were four of them and only one of me. But when I look back on this now, I realize that their reaction was normal and mine was not. I should have been extremely angry about what was being done to me. Those brothers had been expecting me to display some kind of normal reaction to be treated so badly, such as throwing a fit or going out swinging and punching and they were expecting the worst. Maybe I didn't have time to process it because it had all happened so quickly, or maybe the calmness was a kind of defense mechanism I went to. There are other times in my life when people have noticed that I seemed to be extremely at ease in highly stressful situations. My stoic calmness can be a strength in some situations and a weakness in others, and in this case, I don't know which of the two it was.

As I was being escorted to the door, a sister named Debbie snarled, "How did *he* get in here?" She was referencing the Parable of the Wedding Feast and I understood exactly what she meant by saying it. Not only did I not belong to the body of true Christian believers, I was now being carried out of the "wedding feast" and cast away into the outer darkness, forever.

(The Parable of the Wedding Feast is one of the stories Jesus told in the Bible. The story is about a king who gave a marriage feast for his son. The king told his servants invite as many people to the marriage feast as they could find. The servants went and gathered everyone they could find and now the wedding hall was filled with guests. But when the king came in to look at the guests, he saw a man who wasn't wearing a wedding garment and he said to him, "Friend, how did you get in here without a wedding garment?" Then the king said to the servants, "Bind him hand and foot, and cast him into the outer darkness. There men will weep and gnash their teeth. For many are called, but few are chosen."

The reason this man was cast out was because he refused to wear the wedding garment his host provided for him. He chose to remain in his old clothes instead, which was a great insult to his host, who showed his displeasure by throwing the man out. In the parable, the wedding garment represents the righteousness that Jesus clothes us in when we get saved, which is a free gift and is so costly that we could never purchase it ourselves. Jesus meant to show by this parable that a person who refuses to wear this garment of righteousness is despising this gift, which Jesus purchased for us by dying on the cross for us. But in my case, I was no different than any other person in that room, except that I was on the receiving end of the abuse and that they were on the giving end of it. I had not rejected the gift of salvation, I had only not handed in my paychecks. Also, in the parable, the other guests didn't throw anyone out, because it was not their feast.)

I found a rooming house on Chestnut Street that agreed to rent me a room with no money up front. (During this meeting, I handed over my paychecks after I was asked for them and I didn't have them anymore.) The owner of the rooming house told me I could pay the rent at the end of the week when I got paid. That was very fortunate.

While living out, I continued to go to North Philadelphia to gather lambs and to see Dolly and her family. I still hoped she would move in and that after she moved in, I could have a relationship with her.

(Dolly provided the only female touch I received during my 14 year stay in COBU. As a group of brothers and sisters and Dolly and I waited for a bus to go back to the Rescue Mission after being out for an afternoon of witnessing, she was sitting behind me on a park bench and combing my hair. I was surprised that none of the brothers and sisters around me confronted me there, or that later at a meeting, no one accused me of getting a "lamb sister," a 16-year-old girl, "into me" or questioned me about whether I was trying to have a relationship with her. It felt good when Dolly was combing my hair and I became dreamy. I was torn between pulling away because of the brothers and sisters around me or letting it go on. But it felt so good that I just sat there and she stopped when she decided she was done. When I used to visit her at home, I never tried anything.)

When I moved into the rooming house, I had eerie dreams at night. A wave of air, as cold and frigid as death, was flowing over me. Then I was being picked up and carried off the bed. I had to sleep with the light on to keep it from happening. This was the first time I was living out of the church. Being out of the church carried with it the implication that I was soon to be lost to the world, sin and death, so maybe those fears were fueling those dreams, though there may be more to it than that. (In 1994, a year after leaving, I was reading the diaries I wrote when I was in COBU and then I went to sleep and I had the same dream. The feeling was like someone was slowly pulling the bed sheet off me. I was able to open my eyes and see that the sheet was not being pulled away, but there was a wave of heavy cold air flowing over me, then the feeling of being pulled off the bed. It wouldn't happen if I kept the light on.)

One day, a young woman who rented a room across the hall in the rooming house saw me with my Bible and asked me what church I went to. When I told her it was the Church of Bible Understanding, she said, "You're in a cult," adding that her pastor said COBU was a cult. This put me on the defensive. I was certainly not entirely content with life in COBU, but this made me and COBU one and the same. (After leaving many years later, a former member said to me, "So, you finally left that cult." My first reaction was to feel defensive, even though I was now thoroughly convinced that COBU was a cult. It's not always good or helpful to tell someone they're in a cult if you're trying to help them leave it.)

I meet Eric in the library one day. He was an older brother who moved out of the church a long time ago. His sister Lauren was still at the Rescue Mission (and is still in COBU today). I began visiting him and then moved in with him to escape the rooming house. Eric was friendly but he seemed to have ulterior motives, which he admitted to later. He needed someone to pay his rent while he went on a missions trip to Germany. He also sold me his old car and set me up with a mechanic to put a new engine in it. Reggie, the mechanic who was also a live-out older brother, never got around to it. And the car sat in the Rescue Mission parking lot, because that is where Eric set the whole thing up to be done.

Through Eric and his friends, I got out and around to meet people, including brothers and sisters who had left, but who still were loyal to COBU. No one ever spoke negatively about the church. I also got to know Benny and his family, who were Eric's new converts. They visited often, but fortunately for them, they never moved in.

Not long afterward, Stewart put an end to the relationships that sprang up during Open Season. He said that although there was nothing wrong with these relationships, we didn't have a "right society" to present these marriages to. Stewart said that marriage was a social issue and that marriages had to be presented to the society of the church, and that if there was not a right society, then there was no right framework for these marriages to exist in. The reason there was no right society was that the middle brothers and sisters had not accomplished their Christian training in the Retard Course to Stewart's satisfaction. And Stewart warned everyone not to try to make a right society in order to have marriages, because if it were being done for that reason, it wouldn't work. These relationships quickly died on the vine as everyone correctly interpreted the real message, which was that they should end their relationships immediately.

Some may have mistrusted Stewart's motives, yet most believed this line of reasoning. It was done according to the kind of teachings we had learned and accepted in COBU about God, the Bible and human life. It came from our trusted leader whose only motive was concern for our salvation. Stewart was clever. He didn't directly rule against relationships, but instead he went to some deeper level in order to pull the rug out from under everyone in a way they couldn't have control over. **It wasn't a pleasant time, as one by one, these recently-founded relationships dissolved.** I was living out of the church at the time, but I heard about it from my friends there as the information about the most recent breakups came over the grapevine like news reports. Bob and Barb broke up. Until that time, they had a good relationship and others often commented on the love they showed for one another. They both lived in the church for years afterward, but from that time onward they acted as if they had never been in a relationship and they showed no interest in one another and didn't spend any more time together.

Stewart Traill never forbade marriage by telling us we couldn't get married, but he worked hard to create and maintain an environment in which relationships couldn't start or flourish.

Sometimes he asked us rhetorically, "And why aren't the brothers married anyway?" He spoke as if he were merely observing the conditions (such as the lack of a right society mentioned above) and telling us about it. This way, he could forbid marriage while also maintaining the illusion that marriage was allowed. He always said that we weren't faithful enough to Jesus, or that the brothers didn't want relationships because they were afraid of the sisters, or that there was some other fault or shortcoming in ourselves that prevented us from having relationships and marriage. It was our own fault, not his.

In the meantime, I moved out of Eric's apartment and back to 4040 Walnut Street. The brothers who owned the house treated me with the same indifference as last time, but there were more renters in the house now and these people were not from the church, and I was not as noticeable.

Chapter Nine

Moving Back into the Cult
(Doing the Wrong Thing for the Right Reasons)

At this time, I responded to a call for those who were living out of the church to "move back in and to use all their talents for the resurrection." Jim G. was announcing and driving this at every meeting on Stewart's behalf.

All the promising activity in the church had shifted to Manhattan. Most of the activity at the Rescue Mission had ground to a halt and the brothers and sisters there were just going through the motions, going to work every day and not going out to the neighborhoods to gather lambs like they used to. Now there was a resurgence among the older brothers' fellowship in Manhattan and many live-out married brothers were coming to the meetings and building up the church's businesses.

One of the reasons I moved back into the church was that I couldn't fit in anywhere else. While living outside of the church, I could only find unskilled, low paying jobs and the church had a construction and cleaning business in which the brothers worked together. And I had "talents" (as we called them) in things like foreign languages that I could put to use for Jesus and the church. And despite the marriage ban (which I thought was only a temporary situation), I still thought I needed to be living in the church to be able to get married. Becky, one of the sisters I liked, said to me one day when I told her I was still attracted to her that, "I see you as being alone and not united with your brothers." Now that I think of it, she didn't say the attraction was mutual. She only said that I was not following the standards that Stewart taught us about how a brother must be "out front" and "united with his brothers" and "living responsibly in every way before he can even consider taking a sister in marriage." Having little experience in this area in life and maybe also as a result of not having seen an example of a good relationship with my own parents, I thought that these were actual relationship dynamics, at least for faithful Christians, instead of seeing them as rules which were artificially imposed on us from above.

For some reason, I was eager to move back into the church that had cast me out and I was responding to this call from Jim G., the one who led the pack that night I got put out of the Rescue Mission, directing the lynch mob to deal with me in an extreme way over a fault that could have dealt with a lot less drastically. I wasn't living in the church now, so I was free to show up at the Rescue Mission whenever I felt like it and I didn't have to go to meetings if I didn't want to. I had a few friends at the Rescue Mission and I used to go see them. Except for these few friends, the other church members' attitude toward me ranged from indifference to suspicion. But it seemed like it was not possible to find a life outside of COBU.

I also believed in Jesus and in my calling. I still believed that in spite of whatever problems there were in the church and how the number-two man in the church treated me, it was still Jesus's church. I suppose I never examined it thoroughly and except for some minor encounters, I had never been dealt with (that is, abused) directly by Stewart Traill, so I still believed in Stewart's integrity and that he had good intentions toward us. Jim, who was Stewart's deputy, was often rude to me but he wasn't the leader of the church. Jim was being rude to me, that's all, I thought. He's not supposed to be doing it, but I'll just deal with it.

I believed that there was a higher standard of truth and love in the church and I believed that Stewart was kinder and more concerned for us than Jim was. Stewart taught lessons on "loving one another" and he often told us that the way we had treated someone was not loving, so I imagined Stewart to be a loving person, because this is what he talked about. I thought that love was the standard for our lives in the church and that there were just some people in the church who were behaving badly. I didn't realize that it was all really the same thing and I wouldn't know this until some years later. Sure, Stewart had ignored me that time I came for counseling, until I finally got up and left. But he had never publicly abused me or actively mistreated me either. If he had, I might not have moved back in. Even a few years later, when Jim was directing our meetings and giving us a hard time, I thought that if Stewart were here, he would be much kinder to us - not realizing and thinking through clearly enough that Jim, and the "Princeton Sisters" who arrived with him, were sent by Stewart to run the meetings on his behalf and were doing exactly as he wanted. I was to learn this in no uncertain terms later in my tenure in COBU.

(The Princeton Sisters was a term the brothers used for the Gayle Helpers, because these sisters lived in Stewart's house in Princeton. In private, we sometimes called them the "Princess Sisters," which accurately reflected how some of them acted better than everyone else and how demanding and unreasonable they were during meetings when they were acting on Stewart's behalf. Some of them tried to be friendly when doing this job, but others were just obnoxious. We had to be careful how we talked to them, because as Stewart's mediators, to disagree with them meant we were really disagreeing with Stewart.)

These sisters didn't understand business matters very well and in one meeting they were sent to investigate why so little money had come in from the church's business that week. They came up with the idea that if the income reported last week were divided by the number of brothers working and the number of hours each worked, it came to less than minimum wage. And because of this, they said that some of the brothers were going to get put out of the business and they had to get jobs in the world instead.

Joe was able to stand up to Sarah, who was driving this point, by patiently explaining to her that our customers often didn't pay immediately when the jobs were finished, and also that some jobs were still in progress and wouldn't be paid for until they were finished. So really, the brothers were making a lot more than minimum wage. Sarah didn't get the point until the third time Joe explained and really only then because some of the sisters understood now and told Sarah to back off. If Joe hadn't taken the calm and friendly advisor approach, many brothers would have been filling out job applications the next day. This shows the kind of heated and adversarial exchanges that often happened in an environment like ours and the kind of uninformed decisions they could lead to.

It wasn't so great for me living in 4040 Walnut Street because Kevin and John, the owners of the house didn't like me. They viewed me as a strange person, though I did nothing wrong to anyone. I was just someone who kept to himself. But I had no friends there and I thought that if I got into the church's new program, there might be hope for me and my life and that I would be useful, valued, needed and maybe even liked, not that I thought all of this out directly. I thought that my life would have more meaning and purpose, rather than just drifting around and going nowhere.

When I responded to this call, I felt both compulsion and a challenge to do the "right thing." I should have just stayed where I was and not moved back in, but what did I have? A low-paying job and no money for college. I was living in a rooming house run by live-out church members and I felt lonely there. I had no friends. When I talked with the Chinese college girl who rented the room next to mine, it often seemed like she wanted me to come into her room. But I still wanted to "do the right thing" about sex and marriage. My life was a dead-end existence and I was just treading water instead of going somewhere. I thought I would do better and have more hope for my future if I went to Manhattan and lived in the church again. Of course, I shouldn't have moved back in and I was just in store for more trouble. I wasn't a very independent person. I wasn't close to my family and couldn't go to them for help. I was living on a shoestring and not financially secure. Not working toward a degree or a career and not having any focus didn't help. Maybe I liked studying Spanish. That was about it. So, I decided it would be better to do what Jim G. was talking to us about, which was living a motivating and useful life in the church as we waited eagerly for Jesus to return, using all the gifts and talents that God gave us for that purpose, so we could present a gift to Jesus at his return.

Stewart had just published a new series of faith lessons and there were meetings in Manhattan at this time. A lot of the live-out married brothers and sisters were still part of the church and were meeting together and reading these new lessons. These meetings seemed hopeful, while at the same time, it seemed so dead in Philadelphia. So, I made a commitment (as did some others) to move back into the church. Even so, I delayed a while, but whenever Jim saw me, he said, "So, when are you moving in? I thought you said you were moving back in." So, I finally went to

Manhattan and showed up with my meager belongings. After staying at 515 West 47th Street for a few days, I moved to the apartment building the church owned at 162 Woodruff Avenue in Brooklyn.

Most of the sisters who had been at the Rescue Mission in Philadelphia had already moved to Woodruff Avenue, because they could get higher paying jobs in New York. The young sheep were no longer living at Woodruff Avenue, which had been their training center until recently. Stewart had called the leading young sheep brothers together for a meeting and instead of offering the usual encouragement, he ripped them to shreds and told them how worthless they were. The Young Sheep Program folded quickly and nearly all of the young sheep brothers and sisters left the church. And now I was living in Woodruff Avenue with a lot of the brothers and sisters I had been with in the Retard Program (which had been disbanded, without graduates) and now we had all officially become older brothers and sisters. I was no longer under suspicion as an older person and there were no more inquisitional meetings with people being thrown out at odd hours of the night. (Not at this time, anyway.) And there were no more relationships and no one talked openly about relationships anymore.

I had left everything (what little I had) and responded to the call to "use all of our talents for the resurrection." Part of this call to move back into the church was that I should work in the church's Christian Brothers carpet cleaning business. But when I went to a business meeting in Manhattan and stood up at the meeting to say I had come there, as requested, and asked to work in the church business, I was treated with suspicion. Instead of being hired into "The Business," I learned I might be knocking on doors to look for a job – with an ultimatum that if I didn't find a job within three days, I would be put out of the church.

This was typical COBU bait and switch. They wanted volunteers, but when I got there I got conflicting information, to say the least. Jim, who had been reminding me about moving back in and using my talents for God whenever he saw me, was now treating me with indifference and suspicion. Some of the older brothers at the meeting said, "Let him go out and close carpet cleaning jobs." It was a last-minute reprieve. I hadn't been accepted to work with the carpet cleaning crews, but I could go out into the city with a tape measure and business cards to close jobs for the business.

After the meeting was over, I asked a brother where the good places in the city were to go closing. Jim overheard me and said, "Don't tell him anything!" There was to be no kindness or mercy. I was supposed to figure it for out myself. Later, a sympathetic brother pulled me aside and told me to try the Garment District because there were a lot of showrooms there to sell carpet cleaning to, because Market Week was coming up and they would want to have their carpets cleaned.

So now I was on a do or die trial basis as a "closer." After a few days, I had to be taken seriously because jobs were coming in from my efforts and these jobs were being put on the schedule. I continued knocking on doors in the city for the next few weeks and selling jobs, at first successfully and then with diminishing returns, until I was closing nothing, and I became worried. My sales of the first week added up to two thousand dollars, but then it was a thousand dollars the following week, around five hundred the next week and then nothing. No matter how many doors I knocked on, I couldn't sell any more carpet cleaning. I had exhausted the Garment District and moved on to other areas of the city where carpet cleaning was less in demand. I enjoyed the neighborhood feeling of the Upper East side and felt excited by the international flavor of the area around the United Nations, where there were embassies of foreign governments. And it was good to sit down somewhere for coffee and take a rest after knocking on doors for several hours. But I wasn't closing many jobs in these areas. If I were smarter, I would have gone back to the Garment District and started over again.

Maybe I had proven myself enough or maybe more workers were needed in the business, so I got pressed into service as a carpet cleaner. I was happy to be working with the cleaning crews. But I liked those few weeks of going door to door because it gave me a sense of accomplishment at first and it was interesting to walk around the city.

I also "witnessed" a few times when I was out closing jobs. I was carrying a Bible and I saw a young man sitting on a bench, so I went over to talk to him. I resisted the idea at first because I hated the compulsion I felt to witness to people. But the feeling would gnaw at me and I felt like I was resisting God's will if I didn't. It wasn't a problem of being shy. I had overcome that by many hours of witnessing and talking to customers when I first came to COBU. But I may have felt this resistance because I realized that witnessing to people also meant inviting them to come over to the church (though I didn't examine where this reluctance came from, other than it felt like I was resisting God's will).

If I prayed with people and they got saved, inviting them to visit was the next step. I would have asked for their telephone number and started calling them to invite them to the church. But by now I knew what meetings and life in COBU were really like and it wasn't so good for me there. By witnessing to people, I was in effect asking them to come join the church and to live where I was living and to live the way I was living. Knowing what it was really like, how could I be glad about that, as if this were good news that I wanted to tell other people about? I also understood implicitly that anyone who was new to the church would initially be shielded from what life in COBU was really like. They would be treated well at first and they wouldn't find out about the unwritten rules until later. It was a kind of deception we practiced - though to be fair, the brothers and sisters also hoped things would get better and the positive spin we put on things was our own idealized view of the church. I thought the problems we had were just temporary and that in time, things might get better. Things never got better. And in hindsight, this was just the way life was, always had been and would continue to be in COBU - and is today for those who are still living there. I used to think COBU was like the Soviet Union, which had a constitution that, at least on paper, promised all kinds of rights to its citizens, but the actual way of life there was a different story. Yet, despite this awareness, I hung on to my idealized view of the church. That's called cognitive dissonance. This dissonance was to become more extreme over time until I finally realized I needed to do something about it. But at this time, it was not yet to be.

I was also ashamed of myself and my life in COBU, about the way I was treated, about how worthless I felt and somewhere in there, ashamed about how I couldn't have a girlfriend or a wife, because relationships were forbidden. (As mentioned, Stewart said that God allowed marriage and that marriage was a "byproduct of faithfulness to Jesus" but he said that we weren't faithful enough to Jesus to be able to get married.) When witnessing to people, there was a way in which I was saying to them, "Look at me. I have this. I want you to have it too." Even when the press does a story on a televangelist, they're eager to uncover what his life is really like and to highlight the difference between his words and his greed, sexual debauchery and tax fraud, if that is what he's really up to. The non-Christian world will examine your conduct and judge you accordingly. They'll find out about it, if it's there to be found out about. What I mean by this is that it helps if your life lines up with the good news of the Gospel if you're going to talk to others about it. Do you have peace and freedom? Then it can be a joy to talk to others about it. But I was weird and twisted up inside and I was treated with contempt by many of those in the Christian community I lived with (or at best ignored as a marginal person). And I had recently been urged to move back into the church, and when I got there the reaction was, who needs you?

And I was coming to realize, that though we lived with and saw many of the sisters during the day, we couldn't have relationships with them. So how could I be glad about this life, even if in my mind, I could separate the real message of the Bible from the life we lived in COBU? It might have been good, and even fun, to go out witnessing and to proclaim the message of salvation and to pray with people when I first came to the church, when I knew little of what life was really like in the church and had not suffered much yet as a result of it. At that time, I knew little of the Bible except for its basic message and I thought it was good to tell people about it. But now, it was not like this for me anymore and gladness about proclaiming the good news of the Gospel and sharing my new joyful life with others not what was going on inside of me when I felt compelled to talk to the kid I mentioned above, when I saw him sitting there.

I also felt like the whip was going to crack over me if I walked away from this opportunity to witness, because God told me to talk to him, or so it seemed. In reality, I rarely enjoyed the opportunity to witness as a way to share my faith and I wished I didn't feel compelled to do it, because it felt strange to offer someone "freedom in Christ" while I was twisted up in knots and locked in chains. Did I really want to invite people to come live with me and have them experience what it was like to live in the Rescue Mission or to endure the correctional meetings we had with Brother Stewart? And on some level, I also realized that life in the church was mostly about working in the church business anyway. The big drive to use all our talents for the resurrection was really about working in the church business and the money mostly went to Stewart. Not that he was walking around with wads of cash and wearing fancy clothes. The money was used to buy properties, airplanes and other things for the church. As the pastor of the church, Stewart had the privilege of using these things, even if they were registered in the church's name and not in his. Only a small part of the income went to the church's three orphanages in Haiti, though these orphanages were touted as the main reason we were working so hard. The orphanages were started with the profits generated from the Christian Brothers cleaning business when it had been a vast army of willing and unpaid volunteers. Only a small percentage of what we earned went to our living expenses because we were crowded into a few buildings. Food was bought in bulk.

At this time, we used to have meetings in a Holiday Inn near Princeton, New Jersey (where Stewart was living at the time). During one of these meetings, Stewart didn't show up. He left us a message saying that we had excommunicated him because no one remembered to call to invite him to the meeting. For almost a year after this, we had meetings every week in which we deliberated for hours about how to un-excommunicate Stewart and to invite him back. Anyone who said they didn't think we had excommunicated Stewart was told they were wrong. We soon found out that we could never "ask rightly" enough for Stewart to come back. We came up with various kinds of apologies, invitations and committees, but none of it was good enough. We had to rightly ask for Stewart to return, after appropriately facing how we had excommunicated him and having truly repented of it. Really, Stewart wanted to take a break to pursue some other activities. He may also have wanted to use this method of manipulation to make us appreciate him more and feel we couldn't live without him, because of the extreme distress and disruption our alleged excommunication of him was causing among us. At meetings, we could talk about nothing but this for hours. If anyone tried to change the subject there was always someone who, in an anxious voice, would say that we were avoiding the real issue.

After letting this go on for a while, Stewart solved the excommunication problem by arriving unannounced to one of the meetings. He explained that his return was just like what Jesus did in the Gospel of John, Chapter 7, when his brothers invited him to a feast. Jesus answered his brothers, "Go to the feast yourselves; I am not going up to this feast, for my time has not yet fully come." But after his brothers had gone to the feast, Jesus went too, but in private and not in public. Stewart said that Jesus's brothers were playing games with Jesus to get him to make a public appearance, and that Jesus did not want to take part in their deceit. (Stewart, a master of deception himself, was always talking about not playing other peoples' games and not taking part in their deceit.) Stewart said that Jesus didn't lie about going to the feast, because he went for his own reasons and not for the wrong motives his brothers had for inviting him. Stewart said that as a way to re-enter fellowship with us, he had done the same thing Jesus did as a way to set aside our games and deceitful motivations for asking him to return.

Chapter Ten

I Will Work Harder

After a long period of hard work, I got put out of the church business because I was exhausted. There was an intense period of work through the Christmas and New Year holidays. This was always a busy time because of the high demand for carpet cleaning from people and businesses who were preparing for the holidays. Then there was an equally high demand from people who were cleaning after the holidays. This meant a demanding schedule for all of us in the business. We were on the carpet cleaning teams from early morning until late at night. I often came back late to Woodruff Avenue after an evening or night job. Day after day, I lay down in bed and it seemed as if just moments later, the brother in charge of giving out the jobs in the morning was in my room, handing me a stack of job cards with the names and addresses of the day's customers on it. I could hear his footsteps on the stairs and then coming down the hallway before he got to my room, and I felt a sense of weariness and dread at the sound of his footfalls. (There were usually three cards, one each for a morning, mid-day and late afternoon job. Evening or night jobs were added later, when we called in to the office around 5 p.m.)

Then about mid-January, there was a sudden downturn in the cleaning business and any brothers who were not needed on cleaning jobs were sent to pass out flyers on the streets of Manhattan. One day while flyering with a group of brothers, I began to tune out. I stood on a street corner in a daze. I couldn't stay motivated enough to ask each person passing by, "Do you want to have your carpets cleaned?"

I was exhausted after a month of running like a hamster on the treadmill of the carpet cleaning schedule. But in COBU, there was no concept of vacations or even getting a day off to rest. There were a lot of unfilled spots on the schedule now and these needed to be filled with jobs. We couldn't rest on what we had accomplished yesterday. Yesterday's accomplishments were already forgotten. Money had to be brought into the church and this was more important than we were, or than what any of our needs were.

At the next business meeting, the brothers I had been working with that day reported me for being lazy. I don't remember what I said in my defense. I doubt I connected it in my own mind that my "lazy" behavior was because I was worn out. It wouldn't have mattered anyway. The several witnesses who spoke against me were all the evidence that was needed, and besides, everyone else had been working, so why not me? If I had been smarter, instead of standing around with the brothers passing out flyers, I could have walked away, saying that I was going into local businesses to look for customers. That would have helped me escape the boredom of standing for hours on a street corner. But walking away from the watchful eyes of the brothers to take a break in the library would have taken a degree of independent thinking and internal separation from the church that I didn't have at the time. It was also the inertia and momentum of cult life. Because we lived communally and worked in teams, I wasn't likely to break away to take some time to be alone, or to even have that idea occur to me.

(And it would have taken a degree of separation from Jesus, or at least from the Jesus as portrayed in COBU, who hated sluggards and who cast lazy people into the lake of fire, like the wicked servant in the Parable of the Talents who hid his talents in the ground instead of using them for his master. We were also admonished with the words of Proverbs 18:9, "He who is slack in his work is a brother to him who destroys." Stewart said that we were working together with the destroyer (the devil) to destroy the church if we were lazy. This was a serious accusation to bring up against anyone and it often was. Such were the motivational messages in COBU, which were more often negative than positive. Another was that "the devil is prowling around like a roaring lion, seeking someone to devour." This verse in 1st Peter Chapter 5 was written about a period of persecution Christians were going through at the time and is also about the devil tempting people. In COBU it meant that if we let our guard down or slacked off even for a moment, we were immediately backsliding and the devil would devour us.)

This also shows the willingness of church members to cast anyone out of the business, or even out of the church, who didn't live up to the level of work required, even within a few days of not making the grade. It was a militant, do or die way of life. Sluggards were dangerous examples who would infect everyone else with their laziness if they were allowed to get away with it. So, making examples of them kept the others in line.

We often had meetings where Stewart told us how lazy we were and we committed ourselves to working harder. This reminds me of George Orwell's book, *Animal Farm*. In this story, the pigs took over when the owner of the farm died. The pigs didn't do any work, but they were always abusing the other animals for not working hard enough. One of these animals was a loyal and hard-working draft horse named Boxer. Boxer always recommitted himself to the work, saying, "I will work harder." Boxer also said that "Napoleon is always right" (Napoleon was the head pig) and although Boxer sometimes battled his inward doubts about Napoleon's intentions, he maintained that Napoleon always spoke the truth. When Boxer collapsed from exhaustion, the pigs sold him to a slaughterhouse, where he was turned into glue, and the pigs used the money from the sale to buy a case of whiskey.

This may be the symbolic fate of those still in the Church of Bible Understanding who have toiled away for so many years. Although now, with the church's extremely profitable Olde Good Things architectural antique business, there finally might be some sharing of the wealth after Stewart's death. But certainly, any COBU brother or sister who left after years of toil and self-denial has left with nothing as a reward for their labor. Even in recent years, when a sister who lived and worked in the church for more than thirty years was thrown out for "not pulling her weight," COBU sent a sister to represent the church in a court hearing to try to deny her claim for unemployment benefits.

I was in and out of the church business several times. When not in the church business, I got jobs working for "Pharaoh" in the "world." Working for Pharaoh meant not working for COBU. This was a reference to the Israelites' hard labor of making bricks for Pharaoh when they were slaves in Egypt. But really, any brick making I did was when I worked for Christian Brothers Carpet Cleaning. Pharaoh had his limits. I could leave Pharaoh at 5 p.m. and I didn't have to work for him on the weekends. (Sunday was the only day off from the church business, if there was a meeting with Stewart.) The business provided a kind of camaraderie with the brothers I worked with (though many of the brothers were solemn and didn't get into "levity" or "human fellowship," as it was called, and there were certain brothers who acted more like machines than human beings). When I had jobs in the world, I worked with people I didn't know but it was a relief not to be on the carpet cleaning treadmill (which also included business meetings which lasted for many hours, in addition to the long meetings with Stewart). It was even better when I had a delivery job in the world, because I drove a van and was alone all day. I enjoyed jobs like that.

But, there was always a catch. I was not going to rest so easy with my job in the world. Not being "united and working with the brothers" was considered to be shameful (even if I had been put out of the business by those same brothers). With a job in the world, I was less "in fellowship." Although there were no relationships, the sisters seemed to favor brothers who worked in the business a little more. (To get married, according to Stewart and to all those who shared his views, a brother had to be "living rightly in every way, before he can even consider taking a sister in marriage." And not being united with the brothers would be a serious flaw in walking this perfect path toward marriage.) And sometimes shaming tactics were used on brothers about this. For example, a sister walked up to a brother named Warren in the kitchen at Woodruff Avenue one day and asked him why she was supporting him financially.

(When I heard these kinds of questions, especially when different people asked the same question, I knew that Brother Stewart was the source of the question. In this particular case, Stewart told the sisters to say to the brothers, "Why am I supporting you financially?" At this time, the business was not bringing in much money to the church, while the sisters, nearly all of whom worked in the world, had secretarial and accounting jobs that paid well. "Pharaoh" liked COBU sisters because of their honesty and diligence. Some sisters had jobs with a level of responsibility and skill that brothers didn't have and as a result, they were able to earn more than the brothers who worked in the world. Brothers

111

usually had jobs in the world like carpenter's helper or delivery driver - and going to college was out of the question. According to Stewart, if any sister was bringing in more income to the church than a brother was, she was supporting him financially.)

Warren answered the sister's question by saying that he brought in enough money to the church to cover his rent and food, so how was she supporting him? She backed down and didn't continue to press the question with him.

During this time, there were a series of programs such as the storefront and weekend fellowships. We met together in a rented storefront and then went out to the streets to witness for Jesus. Then there was another meeting afterward to judge each other's performance in our working groups. These meetings often lasted for two hours, after we had already been out for two hours. The terms and conditions of the judging were usually humiliating for many, because they would be judged as not having been zealous enough or that they were "holding back." Each group's members reported on one another. This did little to foster trust between us. The weekend fellowships were the same idea, but instead of meeting in a central location, each group selected a nearby town to farm as their own area, with the possibility of starting a fellowship house if the results were good enough. For a time, I was in a weekend fellowship in Elizabeth, New Jersey.

After this, the Church of Bible Understanding started a donation program and our lives were all about this for some time. The underlying concept was that as a tax-exempt organization, the church could receive donated goods, the donors could write off the full market value of anything they donated to us and we could sell these things to make money. The members of the church were a small army of unpaid and zealous volunteers.

We went through several prospective donation managers, who unlike the rest of us in the Donation Program, was going to be a paid professional with experience in management or fundraising, and who aside from Roger, the freelance accountant who managed the church's books, was going to be the only person employed by the church who was not a member of it. Several people auditioned and tried out for the job, but eventually none of them were selected.

One of these prospects was a Haitian man who came to our meetings and explained to us how he was going to manage the program. During the meetings, he took notes in French and English, and also jotted in Chinese characters. I thought he might be accepted for the job because he seemed so brilliant and because the Donation Program was supposed to be for our orphanages in Haiti.

We had one hopeful prospect come on board and stay for a while. It seemed like he was the final choice, but at the meeting where he was supposed to announce his decision, he said that he had given it much prayer and thought, but that he had a check in his spirit, which he said was confirmed by God through his wife as a second witness. (At the time, I thought this meant that the man was led around by his wife, a real no-no in COBU. Really, he just didn't want to insult any of us when he was turning down the offer.) He went out of his way to say what a great bunch of people we were. He praised our dedication and hard work, and he praised Stewart for being a great teacher. But he also seemed relieved about his decision. Many of us were sad to see him go. During the whole time he was speaking, Stewart sat silently and made no comment.

In the meantime, with or without a manager, we had a legion of zealous workers who called potential donors or went out to solicit and pick up donations. Everything was accepted, household goods, outdated office equipment (like old photocopiers) and expired or soon to expire foods. (Including pallets of a new soft drink called Snapple iced tea which had been donated for church use only and was not to be resold, but brothers went out with cartons of it and hawked it to local delicatessens.)

Soon, we had a warehouse full of donated goods, piled to the ceiling. One of the ways to sell these goods was by taking them to local flea markets. Early on Saturday mornings, I went with a crew and a van to the warehouse to pick up a load of things to sell. The warehouse started off with some kind of organization, but it soon became too packed to manage, so we had to climb over the mountains of junk, looking for anything we thought we could sell.

There was a brother named Greg who had the unique skill of making appointments with retail store owners to obtain loads of returned, but still useable, cheap electronics and merchandise. A van full of this merchandise always reaped a good profit at flea markets. What was unique about Greg, apart from his persistence, was his ragged appearance. He wore his clothing until it was threadbare. In colder months, he wore a jacket that was patched up all over with gray duct tape. We often joked that people gave this merchandise to Greg to sell to raise money for the poor orphans in Haiti because he looked so destitute himself. That may have played a part, but it was really Greg's persistence and the unique angle he discovered. A lot of cheap merchandise was returned to stores and the owners of these stores were happy to get a tax write-off for the full market value of this otherwise unsellable merchandise.

Greg took Stewart's teachings about self-denial and about the sin of "looking good" to an extreme. When Greg finally had to request money to buy a new pair of jeans, he later confessed to the brothers at one of our meetings that he was repenting because he had been into looking good around the sisters because of his new jeans.

Later, Greg was removed from his position because Jim G. and some brothers said he was beginning to think too highly of himself and that he was becoming too proud of his success. Greg was summarily removed from his position and forbidden to look for donations again and he was put back on the carpet cleaning teams. There was no justifiable cause for this, other than making sure brothers kept a low opinion of themselves, which was more important in COBU than any financial success Greg was having.

Now, this may seem to contradict the importance of money in COBU, but every now and then, individuals were made into examples in order to set a certain mood. In this case, it was done to knock down a brother who had begun to stand out too much as an individual. Collective success was acceptable, because no one in particular was responsible for it. That way, we could work hard, yet still be told how worthless we were. Greg's success had been completely individual and completely identifiable as his own. No one else was able to work the same angle with the same degree of success. Our other successes were group efforts, such as teams of sisters calling donors. Greg looked tired and threadbare due to lack of sleep, poor nutrition and self-denial, yet he was able to talk his way into seeing the most responsible person in a store or a chain of stores and get permission to come back with a van to pick up a load of merchandise. What Greg did could not be packaged and taught on a mass scale, with success had by all, yet attributable to no one in particular. So, according to COBU logic, Greg had to be sacked. It was grossly unfair, of course.

Stewart told us to take everything anyone wanted to donate to us, even worthless junk. This way, he said, people and companies would get used to donating to us and getting the tax write-off for the fair market value of their merchandise, and they would keep donating and some of it would be profitable to sell. As a result of this, we sometimes became people's free waste disposal service. I went to a dairy company (where one of the brothers worked as a delivery driver) to pick up a storeroom full of cheese, which turned out to be well past its expiration date and very moldy. They expected me to take it anyway. I made a decision, that for COBU anyway, was a daring and independent decision. Rather than being an obedient robot, I refused to accept the cheese. I could have been disciplined and harassed for destroying our connection to this donor. But after first being disappointed and asking me to take the cheese anyway, the business owner seemed to respect my decision. (This was an example of me having internalized COBU principles. One of those principles was "standing on the truth." Because if we took a stand on the truth, Jesus, who is the Truth, would protect us.)

The Donation Program might seem pathetic at first glance, but it was a forerunner of COBU's Olde Good Things architectural salvage business, where old building fixtures are highly valuable and profitable to sell. Olde Good Things pays a certain amount of money to access buildings which are about to be demolished and sends an army of brothers to strip the building of anything sellable, from large marble architectural details to old brass doorknobs. It has a large warehouse in Scranton, Pennsylvania, four stores in New York City as well as stores in Los Angeles, Scranton, Houston and Hopewell, New Jersey. This has become a multimillion dollar business which has **finally allowed COBU to escape relying on carpet cleaning and construction trades for income. In this new business,** the sale of a single chandelier can bring in ten thousand dollars. Much like the Oneida Community, a communal religious sect in New York in the 1850s led by John Humphrey Noyes, a bearded prophet with his own only true version of the Christian faith, the Church of Bible Understanding may be evolving into a purely business operation. The Oneida Community's church business eventually became the Oneida Limited company, one of the world's largest makers of silverware and tableware.

After working in the world while, I was able to get in the wood floor refinishing business owned by Bob, a live-out married brother, where I worked with several other COBU brothers. We were called "The Dirty Dozen" because we were misfits that no one wanted in the church business. We worked long hours and I asked Bob if I could have a short break to go to an art supply store during the day to buy some color pencils and he said, "You have to go after working hours. Even in a job in the world, they don't let you have time off to do your own thing." But we started early and worked into the evening and on Saturdays too. So, **I gave up on the idea of buying art supplies. But soon, I got fired when I** showed up late one day because I went to the bank on the way to work to deposit a 25 dollar check that my mother sent me for my birthday, and because the bank didn't open until 8 a.m., I got to the job site at 8:30. After this, I found a job delivering photocopiers. When I walked in the door to apply for this job, the owner of the business told his secretary not to take any more calls for the job opening, because we found our guy. This job lasted a year and I got to drive throughout the city and the boroughs again. Driving was a nice way to get away for a while. But I was still in the cult mindset, nothing had broken. I didn't think about leaving the church, or not much.

In a sort of roller coaster ride of getting hired and fired from the church business, I was able to get back into the business again. We often had to wait in front of customers' buildings after we finished a carpet cleaning job, because there weren't enough vans to pick up the teams and their machines. One time, we cleaned the carpets for a customer and when she came outside an hour after we had finished, we were still waiting in front of her building and I felt embarrassed. One of the reasons for the limited capacity was that the vans and their drivers were also being used for Stewart's silver recovery business. Stewart concocted a method for removing silver from used darkroom chemicals. Sisters called photo labs to arrange pickups of containers of used fixer, as it was called. Stewart built a huge vat in the garage of his house in Princeton. The fixer was poured into this vat and through some form of alchemy, he extracted the silver from the liquid the way candles are made by dipping a wick in wax. He was now building a stockpile of small silver bars. It was a labor-intensive business with all the calling, pickups and then deliveries of fixer across New Jersey to Princeton, but Stewart had an unpaid labor force who put in 60 to 70 hour workweeks, so it was a low overhead operation.

My downfall came one day, when I was the office dispatcher for the carpet cleaning teams. The teams called in after finishing their jobs and I arranged to have them picked up and driven to their next job as soon as a van became available. In this way, the teams were juggled and somehow the work got done. (Before this, there had always been enough vans and each team had their own van.) At the same time, calls came from the sisters requesting a van to pick up fixer. A sister told me they needed a van to pick up six containers of fixer. I told her I didn't have a van and driver at the moment, but that a van would be available as soon as I could get it. Not long afterward, she called again, angrily demanding why there was no van yet. There was an unspoken imperative in her voice which I understood very well. This fixer business was Stewart's business. The carpet cleaning business was secondary. But, after a frustrating day of trying to manage pickups and drop-offs with limited resources which were also being pushed to capacity with fixer pickups, I said to her, "We're not here to serve your needs." I considered the fixer business as something being imposed on the carpet cleaning business, and that since the business owned the vans, the carpet cleaning teams were a priority. But I was soon to be shown just how wrong I was. I had failed to see what side the bread was buttered on. Although the business technically owned the vans and the sisters calling in the fixer pickups were just being added to the schedule, it was Stewart's business and I had just touched a 600-volt wire. I was asking to be summarily executed at the next business meeting.

We had weekly business meetings where all the brothers and sisters got together to vote on each carpet cleaning brother. Depending on a brother's behavior and whether or not he was pulling his weight, it was decided whether or not he would be allowed to continue working in the business the next week. One by one, we made our speeches and got voted on. I made my speech and I was voted to still be in the business. As I sat back down, I heard a sister say, "But didn't I hear you were fighting with a sister last week?" Another sister said, "Yes, I heard that too."

I was not going to have an opportunity to answer her question. When I began to explain, a brother asked everyone, "Should we revote then?" I asked, "How many agree that I should still be in the business?" In contrast to the unanimous vote minutes ago, only three hands were raised. I sat back down. The same brother said, "Now ask how many don't." I replied, "I already know what the vote is." But I wasn't going to be granted even the small measure of dignity of facing the obvious and just being done with it. "Ask how many don't," the brother said again. So I asked, "And how many don't?" There was a sea of raised hands and complete silence. I had been summarily fired. Most had no idea of what happened that day at the office and no one was going to care to find out. I "fought with a sister." And that was enough.

The following day, after looking at classified ads in the newspaper and spending the day looking for jobs, I remembered what I had done once before. When you don't have much of a job history other than Christian Brothers and odd jobs, you can go to a temporary employment agency and they will put a positive spin on your job history. (And when you fear that if anyone calls your last employer for a reference, which is Christian Brothers, the brother or sister answering the phone will refuse to say anything positive about you because they fear that if they do, they're "taking part in your sin." Or even worse, they might say something bad about you. This was not going to help me get hired, while at the same time, I wasn't going to get away with saying that these poor references were the reason why I didn't get a job, and I might be put out of the church if I didn't get a job in three days). The man who interviewed me at the agency called an electrical supply company and told them he had found them an excellent delivery driver.

I felt like an exile for the next month and was in somewhat of a state of shock after having been summarily ejected into the "world." Until one day, during a period of rainy weather, I was driving along with the window open, enjoying the warm damp air, the misty spray of water on my arm, the rhythm of the wipers and the splashing sound of the tires in the puddles on a bumpy road and I realized I was enjoying myself. I was surprised by this feeling because I wasn't supposed to be enjoying a job in exile like this. But it was a welcome relief to the treadmill of working in the business and the strange interpersonal dynamics with the sisters at the office which was not just because of the fixer business, although that certainly added the element of how Stewart had to be obeyed and worshipped at all costs and woe to anyone who ran afoul of this expectation, even if that meant leaving brothers outside for hours, waiting for a ride.

I was now free from this dysfunctional way of life from Monday to Friday and I was alone and could drive for hours, just thinking. I often had stormy thoughts, especially when I was reviewing the meeting in the Woodruff Avenue basement of the night before and thinking about the way Jim G. treated us. I replayed what Jim and the Princeton Sisters said and came up with rebuttals that would have been great to say, if I had been able to think of them at the time. Sometimes I was going to work after only four hours of sleep because these meetings often lasted until two or three in the morning.

I also began to reminisce about my life in high school before coming to the cult, especially about what summers used to be like. It was the only other life I had known besides the cult and those summers were the best of it. And by this time, I had entered into a full-blown fantasy world about it. This was the first time I began to consider leaving the church and going back to "the world." But good memories alone of my life before the cult didn't have enough force to make me leave and if I even was headed that way, my escape route to home was soon cut off and I was going to have another inducement to stay on and reapply myself to cult life again.

I had begun to visit my father during the last two years. One reason was to enjoy a summer weekend - but I was also checking out my options. I used to sit and watch the summer clouds over the river and wish I could come back there. Sometimes I even prayed and asked God if I could come back there to live. My father had a talk with me on my first visit home from the cult. That summer, he was house-sitting in a big house on the river next to the yacht club. He sat me down on a lawn chair and asked me how things were going. He wanted to know about Stewart and his airplanes and his house in Princeton. I guess he was trying to alert me to the difference between my lifestyle and our leader's lifestyle as a way to show me I was being taken advantage of. I gave him an idealized version of the church, the version I wanted to believe. I told him that we lived communally as a way to save on expenses so there would be money to send to our orphanages in Haiti. I said it could be dangerous living at Woodruff Avenue and that there were drug dealers on the street corners and that sometimes gunfights erupted between them. I told him that one time, a brother was caught in a shootout when he was walking home from the subway. He felt a puff of air from a bullet passing over his head. But God protects us and I feel safe, I added. I told my father that Stewart didn't own the house in Princeton and the airplanes, but that they belonged to all of us and because Stewart was the most responsible brother in the church, he managed these things for the church.

I couldn't see how the older brothers could live in the house in Princeton. We were so irresponsible. The house would probably be run down and dirty in no time, just like the church properties at 515 West 47th Street and Woodruff Avenue. Sometimes I used to go with a crew of brothers on the weekend to do landscaping work at the house in Princeton. The first thing that usually happened when we drove up the long driveway and got out of the van was that three or four sisters met us outside, admonishing us to be quiet, because Stewart was still sleeping. They told us we could only speak in whispers. We weren't allowed inside the house, except to use a bathroom that was accessible by side entrance.

My father didn't press me too much further. He put me on the phone with my mother, who was living in Florida, and she was happy to hear from me. I returned at least ten times over the next two years, usually in the spring and summer. I rode my father's bike around town, took pictures, jogged on the school track and daydreamed about coming back there to live. One time I was out on the bike until dark, riding all over town, just enjoying being there and thinking about how I missed the town I grew up in. I used to arrive at my father's apartment with a small duffel bag with a change of clothing, a notebook and toothbrush. It was like going away on a little vacation from the church. But there was no place for me to stay long term. Every time I visited, my father always told me that there were plenty of jobs in the newspaper and that I could find a rooming house to stay in, if I ever wanted to change what I was doing. That was the extent of the support he was willing to offer me if I left the cult. Sometimes I planned to take the late afternoon train back to the church on Sunday, but by late morning, my father was already asking me if I wanted a lift to the station and I understood that he wanted me to leave. Maybe there was something he wanted to do later in the day.

I would have continued to visit my father, but the woman he was dating moved in with him. I thought that visiting would have been agreeing with adultery. According to COBU theology, if I didn't clearly state to my father that this was sinful behavior, then I was taking part in his sin. This was going to be hard to do if I was staying in his apartment as a guest. So, I decided to stop visiting him. I had been slowly moving toward leaving the church, but now this route had been cut off. At the time, I thought God did this for my own good to keep me from leaving. And soon, Stewart started a new program in the church, which I began to put my hope in. It was another example of being close to leaving and some new "hopeful" program would start in the church which was designed to get us back on track. This time it was going to be a big program and I was going to experience an extreme situation in the church like never before, but this is what eventually cured me of the Church of Bible Understanding.

I left my job as a delivery driver in order to escape the temptations that seemed to be all around. There were days when I could not stop looking at the women who were everywhere in the city. On other days I was completely free from this. Once I looked at one woman, I couldn't stop looking at women for the rest of the day. I tried to avoid this by opening a small Bible and reading it at stop lights instead of looking around while waiting for the light to change. I thought about how unreal this was. I wasn't really reading the Bible because I wanted to read it, but to avoid looking at something. I thought that if I was working with my brothers all the time, I would be free from this temptation. I thought I needed to make a desperate change, and about that time, Bob was restarting his wood floor business, so I asked him if I could be in it again.

Chapter 11

Dreams

During this time, the church bought an entire city block in Philadelphia that once had been a boys' home. It had two large dormitory buildings, a meeting room, a pool, a gym and trees and lawns, with a wrought iron fence around the entire block. We called it the New Property. We began having meetings to talk about who was going move to the New Property for training, but no one was ever voted as being faithful enough to go there, although some older brothers were sent to do guard shifts. Meanwhile, the house in Princeton had been sold and Stewart, his wife Gayle and his entourage of young and pretty Gayle Helpers moved into one of the dormitories on the New Property.

Stewart's quarters were designed to his specifications, which included an office with recessed lighting and a marble tiled bathroom for Gayle. I helped with the renovations in the beginning and one of my jobs was to knock a hole in a wall with a mallet as a way to connect two rooms. I wasn't skilled in any of the trades needed to do the construction, so I didn't keep going to the New Property with the brothers. But I understand it was quite a nice set up. Andrew, the cabinet maker brother, made thirty bookshelves to hold Stewart's library. These bookshelves had glass doors and interior lighting that switched on when the doors were opened. Andrew also had the task of creating a huge U-shaped desk for Stewart. The desk was shaped that way so Stewart could have desktop space at his right and left as well as in front of him. The desk had controls to operate the room lighting and the volume of the speakers built into the ceiling. I learned that Stewart was a picky customer, more demanding than even the most discriminating customers in our business. Stewart complained about even minor imperfections in Andrew's excellent work to a degree that I thought was just ridiculous.

The Gayle Helpers' floor was kept in its original dormitory style. I didn't know it at the time, but Stewart had a private stairway built to access the floor the sisters lived on and he visited their rooms often.

When the brothers had to get together to discuss building a sunbathing deck for Gayle, I became angry because we lived in crowded and squalid living conditions and here we were, going over the fine details on a blueprint for this deck, which would be built on the roof of the dormitory so Gayle could sunbathe (she used to sunbathe nude, I later learned). It was to be built like a greenhouse, so Gayle could use it year round. I sometimes indulged my anger at this difference in living conditions by fantasizing about throwing rocks to break all the glass panes, but I thought that if I did, the church would have me arrested. When the deck was finally built, it was just a wooden enclosure to mask the view from below.

In the meantime, we had to elect a committee to represent us and to meet with Stewart at the New Property to talk to him about some of us moving there. We voted and approved a delegation of older brothers and sisters to go. On the drive there, they began feeling unsure about themselves, so they held meetings at rest stops along the way to vote on one another to see if they still considered themselves to be in a "right spirit." They had two of these meetings on the way and then another meeting in the parking lot of the New Property. At this last meeting, they decided that none of them were in a "right spirit" and that as a result, they were not worthy to meet with Brother Stewart. They got back in the van and drove back to New York.

This odd behavior was a result of Stewart promoting so much self-doubt among us that we considered ourselves unworthy to live at the New Property. What was ultimately behind this was that Stewart didn't want anyone there but himself, his wife and his close circle of young females and a brother to guard the grounds at night. If he wanted us there, he would have just extended us the invitation.

This was a time of hopelessness for me. It was hopeless because I thought it was impossible for me to go to the New Property for retraining. If even the best us couldn't go, what about me? I wanted to be retrained, so I could "use all my talents for Jesus" and to escape the hopeless life I was living in Woodruff Avenue. Maybe I would even have some personal sessions with Stewart where we could review my talents and skills to see how they could be best used for the church. Then I would then be "living my purpose."

At that time, when all looked impossible, I had a vivid and amazing dream that kept me hanging on and gave me hope, despite the circumstances in the church being entirely to the contrary. In this dream, Stewart had repented and was now fully serving Jesus. (An unthinkable concept, how could Stewart not already be serving Jesus?) Not only that, but in this dream, many brothers and sisters who left the church had returned. They were all together in a meeting and everyone was excited and happy.

In this dream, I had left the church and gone home. I was in the house I grew up in, with my father and brothers. My brother took a phone call and told me, "The real estate man said he's going to come and kill you, because you stole his marijuana while you were in his office, and there is nothing you can do about it." So, I was looking out the window, wondering how safe I was there. While awaiting my fate, I began cleaning the sink in the kitchen, when suddenly I was in a meeting at the New Property with over a thousand brothers and sisters! They were all happy and cheering loudly. Brother Stewart was saying, "What shall we get into in this meeting? God's love for you first! And what second?" Nobody guessed. He said he'd give us a clue. He went around the room showing brothers a verse in the Bible. One of the brothers jumped up and said, "I get it!" And he and others headed to the center of the room. (The subject to get into was bearing fruit.) Brother Stewart was lifting up magazine clippings of fruits, holding them up high and then passing them around. The room was full of excitement and Stewart seemed extremely excited, joyful and ecstatic. I found myself laughing uncontrollably at things Stewart was saying and I wondered if it was okay to be so out of control, but nobody was telling me not to act this way. Brother Stewart was saying, "These ones seem so joyful, but you ones living at Woodruff Avenue are so uptight and unreal. It seems like it would be right for you to move here." And then he added, "Since I left the world and decided to fully follow Jesus, I've had no problem with the world. And they know it." ("They" in this case meant the dissenting church members who had left and who were critical of Stewart. They weren't able to deny Stewart's genuine conversion experience and couldn't play games about him anymore.)

In the next scene in the dream, I was following Stewart's wife Gayle as she was climbing a winding staircase in a castle tower and when she got to the top, she jumped out a window and splashed into a swimming pool below. I sat in the window and looked out at the scene below. It was a park. People were swimming and playing baseball. I was wondering if we were allowed jog here. Then I saw a brother, Greg S., jogging, so knew it was okay if he was doing it.

Shortly after this dream, I was guarding the Staten Island house with Greg S. and we went to the local school field to jog on the track. (There was more freedom then than in the times that were soon to follow and we could still do things like jog or play basketball sometimes.) When we finished running, we were talking about the current hopelessness in the church and I told Greg about the dream I had about this wonderful meeting. He said it sounded good, but let's wait and see. I believed the dream. It seemed so real!

In essence, the dream came to pass and it helped me believe what was happening in the church during the next few years. The dream had been personal and directed at me. And I had a tendency to believe that vivid and striking dreams were prophetic messages from God. A half year later, Stewart told us that he had repented and that he was starting over. And soon, many brothers and sisters who had left the church moved back in. Just like in the dream.

I realize now that although the dream foretold what was going to happen, nowhere in the dream was it shown that Stewart's conversion was genuine. But it was still true that Stewart was going to say he had repented (an unheard of and impossible concept at that time) and that many brothers and sisters were going to return to the church and for a time at least, be happy.

But for now, the hopeless situation continued. No one could make the grade to move to the New Property. Then we began to have what Stewart called Backslider Meetings. As a hopeful avenue to our possible repentance, each one of us had to write a notebook journal about how we were backsliders and what we would do if Jesus gave us a chance to start over again. We were allowed to come to the New Property for meetings on Sundays. During these meetings, brothers and sisters read aloud from their backslider journals and then asked all present if they believed they were being honest, and then asked for a vote. Stewart had us make categories among ourselves about whose repentance we trusted and whose repentance we did not trust, with the implication that only those who were trusted were going to be allowed to move to the New Property and be in a restoration program for backsliders.

The biggest change came at a meeting which soon followed. Stewart announced that he had something to tell us that was so important that we must get everyone to the next meeting to hear it. Many ex-members of the church came to this meeting. Most of them were skeptical, but they wanted to know what it was. Stewart said that what he had to say was so important that the universe was going to stop at two in the afternoon on Sunday.

I heard later that there was an ex-member of the church living in Switzerland who went outside and looked up at the night sky to see if anything was going to happen to the universe. (It was night there because of the time difference.) Such is the hold this man has on some people's minds.

Stewart's talk lasted for about two hours. His main point was that he had been making things too hard on himself and that he had been the victim of his own teaching. He claimed that his teaching during all these years as the pastor of the Church of Bible Understanding had essentially been correct, except that he had, in all sincerity, omitted teaching about the grace of God. Therefore, the gospel he had been preaching had been a hard burden on everyone in the church - and even more so on himself. But he said that God had been merciful to him when he overlooked grace, because this omission was not a conscious intention on his part to alter the message of the Gospel.

Stewart never mentioned any of his sins, other than that he had been a little too hard on his wife Gayle recently. He asked Gayle to confirm this fact, and she said that, yes he had been. But she never mentioned anything else he had done, choosing instead to remain silent about it. She could have spoken up when it became apparent that Stewart was not going to give more details about his actions that led up to this meeting, other than to talk about missing grace all these years. Maybe she was hoping he would get to it later in the meeting. Or maybe she had too much to lose by speaking up. Now I realize that those who knew what Stewart had been doing in his private life must have had a different understanding of what Stewart meant to accomplish in this meeting than the rest of us did. I only understood him to mean that he had been driven to extremes by believing in his own teachings (which omitted grace) and that he had been living under a hard and graceless burden, and that as a result, he had treated others roughly, but that ultimately it wasn't his fault. He had been a victim of his own good intentions. And those who lived with Stewart and who knew him the best were confirming his words and were in agreement with him. They had nothing to add or clarify, or to disagree with.

On one hand, it's surprising that no one who knew the real story about Stewart said anything. But, on the other hand, it's easy to say that someone should have spoken up, but this was not easy for anyone to do. I was in great terror when disagreeing with Stewart (whether disagreeing with him at a meeting, or when talking about it to others, because they informed on me). I felt backed against the wall and under great oppression. If Richard Wurmbrand (a faithful pastor who endured 14 years of torture in Communist prisons for his Christian faith) considered Stewart to be a "powerful backslider" and said that he trembled while confronting him, who was I to think I could stand up to Stewart and succeed? The few times I tried and didn't get blasted was not because I exposed his lies, but because he was more interested in damage control. He knew that if he dealt with me harshly after I brought up certain issues about him publicly, church members might think there was some truth to what I was saying about him. So, at these times, letting me slide was his best tactic.

If those in Stewart's inner circle were more aware of what was going on behind the scenes than I was, they were also more firmly trapped by the same forces that kept me in line. What I felt when Stewart was present at meetings and what I experienced by the effect of Stewart's messages during the week and being monitored by the others all the time was merely a watered-down version of the pressure those who lived with Stewart experienced on a daily basis. I didn't live with Stewart. I only saw him at meetings. I also found ways to alleviate the pressure by finding ways to be alone so I could gather my own thoughts and think things over. I found private time when I was alone on job sites. And I kept a journal and began to read books about religion, cults and organizational behavior as a way to find an alternate viewpoint about my situation so I didn't have to accept Stewart's teachings and words as the only filter through which I saw reality and all of life, including my own life, as I was expected to do. Being away from the others was also critical, because Stewart's messages were conveyed through those around me as additional reinforcement of this lifestyle and worldview. Stewart ordered the brothers and sisters to preach his words to one another and to monitor and report on all the others. The power of this system and its control over our lives became an increasingly tightening net as time went on.

What I didn't know then was that Gayle had caught Stewart in a compromising situation with one of the Gayle Helpers. (In a classic case of divide and conquer, Stewart held a private meeting with a small group of live-out married brothers and confessed to these brothers that he had "touched this sister sexually." Stewart didn't tell any of us who lived in the church about this and he never mentioned it to the assembled body of believers at this universally important meeting, in which he seemed to be making a full disclosure about how wrong the course of his life had been until God revealed grace to him and granted him great mercy and a chance to repent and start over.)

When I left the church later, one of the brothers who had been at this private confessional meeting with Stewart told me about it and who the sister was who Stewart said he "touched sexually." This brother also told me that this was the motive behind the "Grace Meeting." Stewart apparently was never clear about what this touching involved, even when making a confession of his sins to these brothers. It could have been anything from one inappropriate touch to sexual intercourse, and perhaps multiple times. Apparently, Stewart had to talk about it and it could not be avoided, because his wife knew. Any other COBU brother who had done the same thing would have had to describe what he had done in complete detail, including the entire history of what led up to it - and he would have to tell all the brothers, not just a select few in a private meeting on the side. Even when I heard about this for the first time, I imagined Stewart may have merely gotten a little too close to this sister over time and in a moment of weakness, he began kissing her and then began to go further and then quickly pulled away, realizing he had gone too far and that he should tell some brothers about it. However, Stewart's behavior toward this sister took place within a system that he arranged and managed, in which he lived with as many as 20 young and attractive females at one time, while denying relationships and marriage to church members. Our living arrangements were dirty and crowded and were almost always in bad neighborhoods, while the living arrangements with Stewart were always in a clean, quiet and safe residential area, so that by contrast, it was always better for the sisters to live at his place. Sisters competed for a place at Stewart's house and as an added incentive, a sister could always be sent back to Woodruff Avenue if she failed to meet the grade. And Stewart often told the sisters to forget the idea of getting married, because the brothers were incapable of marrying them. But he assured them that he would take care of them.

Now as I considered what this brother told me about Stewart touching a sister and even felt the need to be in denial about this touching (Stewart's use of the word "touching sexually" being an attempt to be as vague as possible), I began to piece a few things together. I remembered seeing this sister when she was sent back from Stewart's house in Princeton to Woodruff Avenue during the summer of that year. We were told that she had been trying to get "wrong attention" from Stewart and that because of this, she was sent back to live at Woodruff Avenue. One day when I was on the subway platform, I saw her there waiting for a train. She had always dressed conservatively and the most revealing clothing I had ever seen her wear were cargo shorts that went to just above her knees. This day she was wearing red hot pants, red lipstick and her hair was teased out. She looked like Jodie Foster as the young prostitute in the movie Taxi Driver. She had a disturbed look on her face and she clearly wanted to be left alone. Yes, I thought, she's really into "wrong attention." At that time, I had no idea what might have actually happened between her and Stewart.

So then, the backslider and grace meetings were Stewart's cleverly designed ploy to cover up his own sins and to blend in with and slip away with the crowd. Everybody was considered to be a backslider now and Stewart got us to focus on our own shortcomings, sins and unfaithfulness to Jesus as a backdrop against which he could make his confession and not seem so bad, because there were so many other sinners and he was just one of the many. After all of this focus on our own sins and our gratefulness to be given another chance, we were not likely to pay much attention to Stewart if he was saying he was starting over too, or to pry too deeply into the reasons he said he was starting over, other than the reasons he gave us for it. It may have taken him some time at first, after his wife discovered his relationship with this sister, to develop and come up with idea of having these meetings and then to build up to this big event, which he later called the Grace Meeting, but it had been all been cleverly engineered. All the meetings were now called grace meetings in general and The Grace Meeting meant the meeting where Stewart confessed to having overlooked the concept of grace all these years and we believed that God had revealed grace to Brother Stewart and had graciously allowed him a chance to start over.

Stewart was now hiding within the mass of other sinners and was just a part of the greater restoration movement for all backsliders. We all assumed we were backsliders and none of us challenged this point of view. Being told we were unfaithful to Christ was nothing new and we were used to it, but what was new this time was that Stewart was not ranting at everyone, so no one was defensive about being called a backslider. Look, everyone sins and falls short of the glory of God! Sure, I thought, I'd like to admit I'm a backslider and get restored. The meetings in Philadelphia seemed hopeful now. We called lapsed members of the church to come back and many did. There were more returnees than I had ever seen at any time in the church. Normally, a few people came back now and then to try to start over, bringing their stories of sin and misery and woe out there in the "world" and what their lives were like without Jesus. But this was different.

Stewart wrote several papers and pamphlets about grace and the restoration of sinners and these were printed and given to everyone in the church. This amounted to a promise of great freedom for anyone who believed it, because in COBU, the treatment of people flowed from Stewart's teachings and before this, most everything had been based on absolute militant doctrine and our quality of life flowed down from that. Now, finally, it seemed like the church was going to change. Stewart was stepping down from his place as the absolute tyrant to be a servant of the brothers and sisters. From now on, life in the church would be good and everyone could get along and have normal lives. What I brought away from this meeting was that things were going to change and that it was going to be much better from now on. Stewart even declared that he had been making it too hard for the brothers and sisters to get married and he said it was his fault that no one had gotten married, which meant, in effect, that he was now pronouncing that relationships and marriages were available!

I couldn't understand why some of the former members who came to this special meeting said that nothing had changed. Many of them said it was the same old thing. Hilton, formerly one of the most "out front" young sheep brothers, said that he came, he saw, and now he knew there was nothing to it. Of all people, Hilton would want to start over and come back here, right? And when we began calling ex-members to come back to the church, some of them said they didn't believe that Stewart's actions were sincere because he never called any of them to invite them to a meeting or to apologize for the way he had treated them over the years.

But I didn't process this very well, nor did I understand what these ex-members meant. I lived in. They lived out. It was inertia. The tendency of an object at rest is to stay at rest and the tendency of an object in motion is to stay in motion. Stewart's revelation was not enough to make certain people come back to the church. (Although there were about 80 ex-members who came back to stay during this short period of apparent change. But the majority of those who came to this special meeting sensed the real deal and never came back again.) I was an object at rest, because I lived in. Compared to life in the church before and the way Stewart was before, this was an extreme change. It was wonderful! I, who had formerly been in chains, was being promised freedoms of a kind I had never expected to receive. I was in a happy state of shock!

Actually, it was only a promise to change. Soon the chains were to go on much tighter than they had ever been. When I listen to the recording of this meeting now, it's hard to find anything to have been hopeful about. Stewart claimed to be a victim of his own teachings. He was whining about himself. He said that no one ever tried to tell him anything or tried to correct his errors over the years. When a sister named Diane asked, in a reminding sort of way, if there hadn't been a few people who tried, he yelled at her. So she sat back down and stopped trying to talk to him about it. What I was responding to in Stewart's talk was the idea that he could admit that he had been wrong about anything. It was the first time I ever heard him say it. He was no longer trying to portray himself as infallible. After hearing this, I believed things might change.

Another comparison I like to make about the reactions of those who lived in and those who didn't live in the church is from a book I read when I was in COBU, called *Escape From Colditz*. (There probably was a reason why I liked books like that.) During World War II, the Germans put Allied prisoners who had made unsuccessful escape attempts in a castle. While it seemed impossible for anyone to escape from there, there was now a concentrated population of prisoners who were experienced in escape methods. And escapes happened frequently. A group of prisoners who were about to escape through a tunnel were advised that when moving across the fields at night, they should jog slowly instead of walking, because if they were walking and someone shouted to them to stop, they would freeze in their tracks. But if they were already jogging, they would start running even faster. In the same way, those living outside of the church were aleady in motion and most of them were not going to quit their jobs and move back in after hearing Stewart's "important" message. But I lived in the church and when I heard it, I thought it was amazing and I stayed for more.

I was in a state of bliss for the next three months. But I woke up one morning in a state of shock. It had taken me that long to process the actual significance of Stewart's words. It was as if a trusted friend told me he cleaned out my bank account and stole all my belongings, but he said that he was sorry now that he had done it. Because Stewart seemed so remorseful - and because the news of this robbery was so unexpected - I was mostly thinking about how he was asking for forgiveness. But later, I thought, "He did what?" I had been bankrupted and cheated out of ten years of my life by a false teacher, who now admitted that, besides being the greatest victim of his own teachings, that some of the effects of his wrong teaching have trickled down to me and that I may have been affected by it!

Stewart soon shifted the attention away from himself by creating a diversion. He said that an unfortunate side effect of the brothers being set free by grace was that the sisters were extremely angry, because until then, they had been in complete control of the brothers. And now, he said, they would do anything they could to take back that control. We all knew, because Stewart taught us for years, that women want to be in control. (Stewart said that the brothers had been held down by the heavy burden of his graceless teaching until now - a burden which did not come from the sisters, by the way.)

This was a double-edged sword. Stewart was saying that the brothers were doing well now. We were faithful to Jesus, strong and united together and thankful for what Jesus was doing for us. Stewart was coming to the brothers' meetings and acting as if he were one of us. During our voting, he even asked to be voted on. (We voted on which brothers we saw as doing well and which were not doing well. These ones were supposed to get help.) The brothers were happy when Brother Stewart asked to be voted on. Stewart asked us if saw him as being in the faithful category and a brother named Jeff was ecstatic with joy that Stewart would even ask such a question. All the brothers felt encouraged. Kevin was at that meeting, having returned from several years of drug addiction. (At this writing, Kevin is the second in command in COBU.) Others like him had also come back. Their health was improving too.

Ah, but those sisters. Stewart said they were unhappy about all of this new freedom. They were in a rage about losing their control over us. We had the upper hand now and as the Bible says, men are to lead. Stewart said that the sisters' rebellion against the brothers was really a rebellion against Jesus himself. Scenarios like this were a part of the worldview we adhered to. Stewart always portrayed any wrong behavior in absolute spiritual terms, so that a person was either on the side of God or on the side of the devil. All of our actions had eternal consequences, because in the end, all of humankind would be divided between the faithful (there weren't going to many of those) and those who had rebelled against God, who would now be brought into submission, but then it would be too late for them to submit willingly. Their fate was to be cast into the lake of fire, which burned forever and forever. Stewart was a master at portraying life on this stage, so that our actions had eternal consequences. Usually what had negative eternal consequences were any of our thoughts, ideas and actions which were not in line with the agenda that Stewart was promoting at the moment. It was powerful stuff, and very effective.

Despite our new freedom to have relationships and marriage, now with this new revelation about the sisters, relationships didn't seem possible. I wondered how I could marry a woman who was in rebellion against God and who was trying to bring the brothers, and me, down. Stewart told us to ask the sisters, "When are you going to turn from your rebellion and stop trying to bring down the brothers' fellowship?" There was a sister I liked and when I got a few moments alone with her, this is what I believed she was doing, although I couldn't see any specific evidence of it in her behavior at the moment. But I believed what Stewart told us, so I told her I liked her, which I was now free to say to her, but I also told her that we couldn't start a relationship if she was in rebellion.

So, you see, Stewart didn't forbid marriage, but he always said there was some problem preventing us from having relationships, which he was pointing out to us as if he were merely observing it and telling us about it for our own good. Really, he created these scenarios to pit the members of the church against one another, in this case, the men against the women. During this time, many sisters left the church. Meetings at this time always included a session in which the sisters had to try to prove they were no longer in rebellion, and they were always never believed. The fact that they looked disturbed and upset by this unfair treatment was used against them as proof that they were in rebellion. If they disagreed, this was considered as fighting against what everyone was saying about them, and fighting is rebellion. So, it was a double bind. The sisters had to either agree that they were in rebellion, or disagree and have their disagreement used against them as proof of fighting against the truth. Sisters made commitments about how they were going to stop rebelling and nobody believed their sincerity. This treatment went on for about a year, until Stewart decided to put pressure on a different group in the church. So, at one meeting, he summarily declared that the sisters were no longer in rebellion.

Stewart now shifted his attention to the middle brothers and new disciples. During this time, we began taking in large numbers of homeless people. There were hundreds of people sleeping on the floors at night in the train and bus stations in New York City. One night, the brothers went out and brought about 40 people back to Woodruff Avenue. I was sick that night, so I stayed in my room. Someone came up and told me to go downstairs, because a miracle had happened and that "Jesus brought in a lot of new brothers." I went down and saw the crowd in our basement. It was like a miracle. Almost nobody new had come to the church in a long time and certainly not in numbers like this. This was the beginning of an all-out effort to bring new people in.

But over time, these new people among us became unruly. We never worked out a systematic way to provide care for them. We had no facilities and we were not a homeless shelter, a rescue mission or anything of the sort. Just a cult that saw the possibility of exploiting homeless people for free labor. Now, this is a little extreme to say. The brothers tried to help these "new disciples" and we talked to them and read the Bible with them. It helped me to change my view of homeless people and who they were and what they were like. Many of them had decent lives at one time, but for various reasons, whether addictions or unemployment, they became homeless. Some of them were good to get to know and I became friends with them, as many of us did.

But there was a job to do and Stewart didn't consider any of the homeless people as someone to get to know. Although Stewart attached eternal consequences to all things, he was not very concerned about anyone. I gradually came to realize that the church was merely an income gathering machine to support Stewart's lifestyle and that gathering new people had economic, and not eternal purposes. Stewart sometimes said so himself, that we should gather more people to have more workers. Ultimately, the Christian training we offered was a way to winnow out the unwilling and to find those who were obedient and trainable, and to keep them in submission. Biblical doctrines such as serving others and giving up our lives in this world served as reasons to give up everything to serve the machine. People were expendable. If they didn't want to obey, you could always find someone else.

The church also was Stewart's captive audience and the stage upon which he could play the role of The Great Bible Teacher. The basic script and underlying plot which never changed, although there have been various changes in the script and the supporting cast, was that Stewart was the only true Bible teacher, now and for all time, because no one since the time of the Apostles had known the real truth. Sometimes Stewart cast doubt on whether the Apostle

Paul (who wrote much of the New Testament) knew what he was talking about. Sometimes Stewart let us know that all other Christians since Paul's time had gotten it wrong and that the truths he was teaching us had not been revealed again to the world since the time of the Apostles, because the truth had been lost and forgotten during the intervening centuries. Stewart would then launch into some convoluted discourse about how "faith is godly thinking," or some such thing, telling us that no one else has ever known this.

I understood that when Stewart announced that no one else knew his new teaching except for our church, this meant that if Stewart had told it to us only just now, that until a few minutes ago, he considered himself to be the only person in the entire world who knew the truth forgotten since the time of the Apostles. Stewart said that the truth had been lost, not because of the Dark Ages, but because Christians throughout all history had been rebellious. Rebellion was a major theme in Stewart's teaching. Stewart was the faithful teacher in a rebellious world - and the pastor of a church whose members he was constantly calling out on the carpet for being rebellious too. If one group in the church wasn't rebelling at the moment, another part of the church was. And that's why there could be no relationships or marriage. Stewart was a master at creating artificial crises and portraying our situation as being so urgent and desperate that there was no time for any kind of normal life or even to think about having a normal life. He said we were supposed to break up and put to death our lives in this world. Stewart's favorite crisis was, "You're going to die in two seconds and be cast into the lake of fire." He created life-threatening spiritual emergencies that left us scrambling desperately for the slightest thread of hope of being saved, with no time to consider anything else. Our meetings and our lives were increasingly centered around this storyline after the so-called Grace Meeting, as Stewart turned up the dial on the flames of hell at every meeting and with every message to the church throughout the week. And what was not covered by this was occupied with long hours working in the church businesses, gathering and managing new converts and meeting to vote on how we viewed one another's level of faithfulness and obedience to Stewart's messages.

In my last years in COBU, I came to understand that if we accepted Stewart's claim of having this unique insight, it put us under extreme obligation to him, because he was the only teacher who knew the truth. God was only showing Stewart these things, so now the stakes were raised to eternal proportions. God couldn't show other teachers the truth, because according to Stewart, they were all either extremely arrogant or in rebellion against God, so those teachers weren't able to help us. So, we needed Stewart.

And if our great leader, who was the only one able to understand these biblical truths, also said that we were rebellious and headed straight to hell, it was incumbent upon us to accept the cure he offered us as a way to escape our condition, since all the other blind teachers (other than Stewart) could neither identify our rebellion, nor could they help us even if they were aware of it. And if our leader had demands on our time and on our very lives? And if, while not directly saying he prohibited marriage, he spoke about conditions within us (such as rebellion) that were preventing us from being able to get married, wouldn't we accept his diagnosis and work on the cures he proposed for these problems so we could eventually have marriage? Ultimately, Stewart held the keys of life and death, of heaven and hell. Really, only Jesus holds those keys, but we needed true revelation, especially in these last days, and Jesus was only showing the truth to Brother Stewart. We couldn't receive any revelation from God on our own because we were rebellious, so God was not going to show us anything. But if we admitted to our rebellion and accepted the cures that Stewart proposed, we might have a small ray of hope. This is why it was hard for me to believe that God could be showing me anything. For example, when I read the Bible and it didn't line up with what Stewart was telling us, or when I doubted Stewart's solutions to our problems. I sometimes doubted that the problems he said we had were real and I considered the cures he proposed for them to be worse than any disease he said I had.

Chapter Twelve

The Criminal Element Takes Over

The new people we took in off the streets were often unruly, and in many cases, it was our fault. During one of the meetings at the New Property in Philadelphia, the new people took over and a riot was about to happen. There were several men walking around with boards in their hands. It must be noted that Stewart wasn't a coward and he didn't leave the room. None of us did. We tried to contain the situation. As a great manipulator, Stewart had a good knowledge of human behavior because it is not by accident, but by design, that people are controlled. Although many of us were afraid that this crowd was about to go in to a rage, Stewart knew that in any crowd, there are only a handful of people who are stirring everyone else up and that most of these people, as rough as some of them appeared to be, didn't want to fight or hurt anyone. He realized who the trouble makers were, usually the ones with something in their hands, and he directed the biggest and strongest older brothers to "talk to them," which meant to surround them. If the brothers had pushed or tackled any of these men, the others might have been incited to riot. But through the careful use of dialog about "helping people," Stewart was able to manage the crowd. Most of them had legitimate gripes about their treatment, but they weren't violent people. Their part in this whole scenario had been mostly to shout and yell.

Stewart also carefully played both sides of the crowd and let the new people vent about which older brothers always mistreated them, even though these older brothers were the ones who carried out Stewart's orders and policies on the new people. It was more convenient to have the older brothers seen as the oppressors for the moment and for Stewart to appear to care about them and to allow them to voice their dissatisfaction as a way to wisely play the crowd and to let them vent their anger safely.

As part of the church's donation program, trainable new disciples were sent out with pushcarts to sell donated items. And other groups of new brothers, often led by an older or middle brother, or sometimes by an older sister, took vanloads of donated cans of paint to sell on street corners. Stewart saw the potential of combining unpaid homeless labor with free donated goods to generate income through the donation business. Profits were high, because there were no inventory or labor costs and workers lived cheaply in group living situations. If this worked, Stewart could get rid of the older brothers, many of whom had been in the church for twenty years. There were many reasons for this move. We knew too much about Stewart and how he operated. And despite our extreme self-abnegation, homeless people would expect even less reward for their work than we did. Also, as the older brothers grew older, they would soon be incurring medical expenses, not to mention expecting some kind of retirement. Maybe it was time to push the older brothers out now.

Whatever the underlying reasons, Stewart seemed glad to have found a way to get rid of the older brothers. He said he was tired of us and that he was glad to finally be able to get out from under the "iron fist" which he accused us of ruling the church and the church businesses with. He accused us of wanting to remain in control by not training the new people to move into positions of responsibility. In reality, most of the new people were hard to train and many of them couldn't be trusted on jobs, because they stole from our customers. The older brothers didn't steal money, jewelry or prescription medicine from our customers' homes. All of this happened frequently with new brothers, and we were careful to get to know and then select the ones who didn't steal and who could be taught how to use the carpet cleaning and wood floor machines. Some new brothers could be trained, but the number was far less than what Stewart might have expected.

One day, I had a van and a carpet cleaning machine and young man named Trevor as my helper. When we left a job and were on the way to another, he asked me if I knew what a certain word meant. He pronounced this word as "liar." I thought that maybe he had been reading the Book of Psalms in the Bible and had encountered the word "lyre," which was the musical instrument David played, and that he didn't know how to pronounce this word. "Are you asking about the musical instrument called a lyre?" I asked. No, that wasn't it, he said. "How is it spelled?" I asked. "L – I – R – E," he said. Now I suspected he had picked up some foreign currency at the last job. I said, "Oh, you mean *'lee–ray.'* That's the kind of money they have in Italy. It's not worth very much, a thousand *lire* is worth about seventy-five cents." At that point, seeing that he hadn't struck it rich after all, Trevor showed me a couple of crumpled bills, which amounted to 4,500 *lire*. This was only petty theft, but you see, a new disciple had been willing to take what he thought was about 4,500 dollars from a customer. He had not been able to contain his curiosity about what it was worth. And now that he found out, it was suddenly worthless to him and he didn't even mind letting me know he had taken it. This is just one example. New brothers also stole jewelry and other things. So we had to be careful about who we took on jobs.

But, Stewart now declared us to be the "ex-older brothers," claiming that we were rebellious and no longer worthy of being called older brothers. Then he began a move to put us out of the church. This had disastrous consequences and it didn't work. And some people almost got killed because of it.

There had been "sister purges" before this. The most notable being when Stewart slammed the sisters for a year after his so-called repentance at the Grace Meeting, probably to keep them on the defensive so they couldn't say anything about his inappropriate conduct toward some of the sisters. If they had spoken up about it, it would have just appeared as if they were fighting back and it would look like the very rebellion he was accusing them of.

(Some of us who were familiar with the writings of Alexander Solzhenitsyn compared the purges in communist Russia that he wrote about in his book, *The Gulag Archipelago*, to what was happening to us in COBU. A brother named Peter first used the word purge to describe the onslaught of abuse that Stewart directed at specific groups in the church and I understood where Peter was coming from when he said it. And soon, others who didn't read Solzhenitsyn's books started using the word. After meetings that began with Stewart's angry tirades, but turned out not to be so bad, the brothers sometimes said, "I thought it was going to be another purge." But until now, Stewart had never tried to drive anyone out of the church with the degree of ferocity he was directing at us. (Though people who were in the church before I was have said that Stewart did the same thing when he divorced his first wife and married Gayle, assassinating the character of anyone who disapproved of his actions and many left the church at that time.)

The church was renting a building at 810 North Broad Street in Philadelphia to house the large number of new disciples who were being brought in. The building had only the barest essentials and wouldn't have passed any regulatory board's requirements for a men's shelter. There was no kitchen at "810," as we called it, and there was only one shower. The Church of Bible Understanding flew under the radar in these things. People were put in warehouses that were converted into living quarters. Yet, there was some success, if it could be called that. New people were swept up and they seemed to be doing well "in Christ," because many of them responded to Bible teaching, a place to live and some concern on our part.

But now Stewart wanted to sack the older brothers. This started at a meeting where Stewart used Jay as an example of what was wrong with this new operation at 810. Stewart admitted there was success with the numbers of people being brought in. But he said there was a problem. The new brothers liked Jay. This was an intolerable situation, because according to Stewart, being liked set a wrong example which gave the new people a false idea of what Jesus was really like. New brothers considering older brothers to be their friends disrupted the flow of command from Stewart. The older brothers were only supposed to be conduits of Stewart's communication and control and they were not supposed to get in the way of that communication or to modify the message in any way, such as by being considered friends. (In my last year in COBU, I read a book about cults which described this process very well. The book explained how cult members were removed from their positions if they became anything other than channels through which the leader controlled and trained new converts.)

So, without actually stating it as such, Stewart was accusing Jay of not being a proper channel for his influence on the new disciples. When the new brothers at 810 spoke up to defend Jay, Stewart would hear none of it. Jay continued to defend his position for a while, but he saw the writing on the wall. Then Stewart told Jay to execute himself, which meant that Jay had to explain in his own words that what he was doing wrong and why he agreed with Stewart (even if he had disagreed with Stewart's indictment against him until this moment). Stewart often used the technique of having a person explain the charges he made against them in their own words, for two reasons. First, we weren't allowed say that Stewart was forcing us to do something, because we weren't allowed to blame him for anything. And second, because a brother had to give his own reasons why he agreed with Stewart, this could be used on him later if he changed his mind about his confession. Stewart would call him liar because he had agreed to the charges Stewart made against him and had given his own reasons for why the charges were true.

Over the years, most brothers and sisters were trained into this technique and they capitulated almost immediately at the first sign of this treatment because they knew Stewart would go on as long as necessary until they gave up. He brought in others as witnesses against a brother and if the brother still disagreed, Stewart (and the others in the crowd who were shouting at him) told him he was "fighting against the truth." This was used as evidence against him, because fighting against the truth was wrong. One of Stewart's favorite tactics when he got the crowd on somebody, was to refer to the crowd as the "body" (meaning the body of believers, who were the body of Christ). He asked the dissenting brother if he were so smart and so arrogant that he believed he could see better than the sight of the entire assembled body of believers. So now the brother was disagreeing against the body of Christ, which meant he is in disagreement with Christ himself. And it was rare that anyone in the crowd would defend the brother on trial. If they did, Stewart would put both of them on trial, and continue the same process against both of them.

In my last years there, I saw the new disciples undergoing this same process which Stewart used to break their wills and I saw their reaction to it when was used it on them for the first time. By watching this, I understood now that the same processes had been used to train me to be obedient when I first came to the church. Stewart's methods were all-encompassing and had the effect of pulling the rug out from under me, leaving me with no ground to stand on. Even when it was not being done to me, I saw it done to others. It was effective in training us to be obedient even if we were just watching it being done to others, because it taught us that we could not overcome Brother Stewart.

After Stewart removed Jay and the other older brothers from being responsible for managing the operation at 810 North Broad Street, he soon moved on to strip all of the older brothers of what power and privileges we had. He made courtroom-style charges against us at meetings. He set the sisters up to decide about what should be done with us. He introduced the moves he wanted the sisters to make by asking them questions that contained an embedded command, like, "So, do you think the older brothers should have their money handling privileges removed, or should they keep them?" The sisters talked among themselves and then took a vote and it looked like they were doing this to us and that Stewart was just asking questions. One of the outcomes of this process was that all of the older brothers were removed from positions of responsibility in the church and the new people, many of whom had been living on the street only weeks or months ago, were put in charge.

Many of us were sent to other locations in the church. The worst place to be sent to was 810, because it was now entirely under the control of the new people, who had a committee and reported to

Brother Stewart on the older brothers' words and actions. When I lived at 810, I was ordered by the new people not to talk to another older brother, in order to not be taking part in the "conspiracy" and the "wrong agreement" that Stewart accused us of having.

(Stewart often used the tactic of accusing us of taking part in a conspiracy. When a brother protested and said that we had never gotten together to plan a conspiracy, Stewart said that we didn't even have to talk to one another to plot these conspiracies, because they were in spirit. Stewart accused us of having a "murder-suicide pact to poison the new disciples" and he said that Woodruff Avenue was our "country club," and that we were living there "on a hotel basis," despite the building being in a state of disrepair and being located in a violent neighborhood.)

When the vote was taken about where to send the older brothers, I was voted on to move to the Lamb House in Philadelphia. I was glad I didn't have to move to 810 because I heard about how it bad was there now that the new disciples were in charge. If I had known in advance that I was going to 810, I might have left the church. I had nowhere to go that wasn't a move out of desperation, like spending the night on the subway or in the park (as brothers did sometimes, but came back after a night). Maybe I would have called my mother and asked for money for a ticket to Florida. But there were a lot of barriers within me to doing that. But, I don't think I would have gone to 810 if I had known ahead of time.

Stewart described this move as being for our good. He said that the older brothers were in such a hopeless spiritual condition that our lives had to be broken down. Any social life between us had to be broken apart because he said that any time we got together, we did our "dinosaur thing" because that was our nature and we couldn't change it. (Stewart called our way of relating to one another "the dinosaur club," meaning that we were old and set in our ways and that there needed to be new leadership in the church.) Stewart made it sound as if he was extending a last-minute offer of help, an olive branch maybe, after raging against us and talking about our depraved condition for such a long time. He seemed to be just making an observation about our condition and although he had decided at first that we were hopeless and that we should be driven out of the church, he had now found a way to help us. (This was another one of Stewart's common tactics. First, he beat us up and then he acted as if he had discovered a way to help us.)

So, I was going to the Lamb House, a church residence in Philadelphia. It was not too bad of a place. I would be able to leave Woodruff Avenue in Brooklyn, a violent place where there were frequent gunfights on the street and where we lived in crowded and dirty conditions. The night before we loaded ourselves into a church bus to Philadelphia, I dreamed I was in the front hallway of the Woodruff Avenue residence, talking to new brother named George. In this dream, I told George I had been voted to move to the Lamb House, but George said, "You're not going to the Lamb House, you're going to 810!" And then he began to laugh with wicked delight and his laugh became louder and louder until it was a roar. Then I woke up.

It was just a dream and I forgot about it. I felt happy when I piled myself and my few belongings into the bus with the other older brothers who were moving. As the bus drove away, I looked back down the street one last time and shouted, "Good riddance, Woodruff!" I hated that place. I thought I was being sent to Philadelphia for retraining and spiritual restoration, but really, I was heading for another round of abuse.

When we got to the Lamb House, I walked up to a room on the second floor. I put my duffel bag down and stood looking out the window at the view of a lawn surrounded with tall oak trees. This was much better than the violence and noise of Woodruff Avenue and I hoped this could be my room. This was too good to be true, by the way, as you'd never get a room with a view in COBU. I left the building and took a walk around the neighborhood. I always liked the Philly vibe, with the long blocks of little brick row houses and the mom and pop delicatessens on all the corners. I had lived there in 1983-84 when I was in the church and it brought back memories.

When I returned to the house, there had been a message from Brother Stewart asking what all these older brothers were doing there. And specifically, what was Jim LaRue doing there? (Although it had been decided in a meeting that all the older brothers couldn't move to 810, so we were divided up among several locations in the church. I envied the few who were sent to the Staten Island house where divorced and separated mothers lived with their children in a lifestyle that was, although communal, relatively suburban.) There were some new brothers standing around, with looks on their faces that seemed to say, we don't like you weird "ex" older brothers. Stewart told these new brothers, "Tell these ones to get to 810 immediately to be with their other ex-older brother dinosaurs!" So, there it was. I had been tricked into moving to Philadelphia under the pretext of living in a somewhat nicer and less violent place and upon getting there, after a brief walk around the neighborhood (where I began to have an increasingly uncomfortable feeling that something was amiss), I was ordered to move to 810 immediately.

I slept the first couple of nights on the ground floor of 810, which used to be a pizza shop. There were still hand-painted murals of Italy on the walls, but the booths had been ripped out and everyone slept on the floor. The homeless men who were brought in off the streets had to sleep on the street level at first until it could be seen who was trustworthy enough to stay. As part of our punishment, the older brothers were supposed to sleep only on this floor, but I soon moved to the fourth floor there was a long open room filled with rows of beds.

With the older brothers no longer in charge, 810 North Broad Street was not being supervised as well as it had been and soon, the criminal element took over. Claude and Robert were two of the new disciples I got to know, because they were also sleeping on the fourth floor and I used to talk to them sometimes. They told me they used to be in the Junior Black Mafia. I didn't believe a lot of these guys when they told me their stories. I thought they were just making things up. Robert said he still had his gun in the trunk of his car, which was parked across the street. He said that since he had become a new convert to Christ, he just hadn't had the time or opportunity to get rid of the weapon, but he intended to, really soon. I was so worn out by continual work and constant abuse that much of this didn't register and it just sounded like nonsense. Did Robert really have a gun in his car? Did he even have a car? I don't know.

One night when we were all sleeping, Claude left the radio at the side of his bed turned on. I got up and turned it off. In the morning, when Claude found out I turned off his radio, he told me to never do that again. He wasn't specific about what he might do to me if I did, but it did seem like I would regret it if I ever tried. Until then Claude had always been friendly to me. He talked to me about what he used to do when he was a gang member. And he told me that Robert had a bullet in his lower back that doctors were not able to remove for fear of damaging his spinal cord and that the lead in that bullet was slowly poisoning his blood.

Later we found out that Claude, Robert and some others had been selling drugs from the building and bringing in prostitutes when we were asleep. There was a certain amount of cash sent to the house, which they had control of and were using for these purposes. There wasn't much food available because they were selling the food as well. Remember that until recently, this was the building that Jay and others had been running so well (at least in COBU terms) until Stewart removed them from their positions when he found out that the new disciples liked and respected the older brothers. There was soon a replacement leadership and it was not good. They were good at fronting with Brother Stewart that all was going well. And the reason they wanted me and some of the older brothers to sleep upstairs where they stayed (instead of on the first floor, where I was supposed to be sleeping on the tile floor) was for protection. If older brothers were there, then no one else was going to snoop around in the rooms and take their things. For all I know, those things were the weapons and drugs they kept around. They told me they knew that the older brothers wouldn't steal anything, because we were honest and trustworthy people.

There were some new brothers who liked me because they saw Stewart getting on my case and sometimes I stood my ground, and they respected me for that. Older brothers like Chuck and Kevin pushed them around all the time, but they never stood up to Stewart, so they didn't respect those brothers. This was a dubious respect to earn. It was the kind of respect they had for those who stand up to "the man."

One of my friends there was Charles, who surely knew of everything that went on in the place and selectively revealed certain details to me, while hiding things he figured I shouldn't know about. I also let him call me "the German," which was Stewart's favorite epithet for me. That name came about when I lost my cool at a meeting and I complained about the treadmill existence in the church and about Stewart's teachings about denying and killing off our human desires and interests. I had a German textbook in my hand and I waved it over my head and said, "I hardly have time to study anything. Here, it says German Made Simple! It feels like such a sin for me to read this!" Stewart told me that I shouldn't be studying German at all. And from that point on, he refused to call me by my name. I was now "The German Student," or simply "the German." While this is not a bad name in itself, I realized that Stewart was disrespecting me by refusing to use my name when talking to me and that he was referring to this incident as a way of defining me to the others. So, the first time Charles said "Hey, German!" to me, I was annoyed, but then I realized he was just being friendly and that it was a sign of respect, because I was the guy standing up to Stewart and of course Charles would use that name for me. Stewart reserved the truly derogatory names those among us who were the high achievers and out-front personalities, whom he labeled as the "celebrities." These were the brothers that most of us depended on for leadership or whose opinions we trusted, sort of a second layer of leadership under Stewart. Those brothers were Chuck, Jay and Kevin and some others. In their case, Stewart used nicknames which directly negated their masculinity. Stewart called Jay "Squishy."

The fact that expenses and receipts did not reconcile was the reason Robert, Claude and the other new disciples got found out. The older brothers at 810 no longer had control over money. And if we sensed anything was going on, we were not going to talk to Stewart about it. Stewart came over from time to time and had pleasant talks with these people and urged them to get on our case and keep watching us, but he didn't want to hear anything from us.

One time when we were assembled together, I tried to say at least something about the way it was there. Stewart replied, speaking to the others about me, "We don't want to hear what this dead man has to say." (At this time, it wasn't yet entirely clear to me whether Stewart was speaking for God, or whether he was just a cult leader. The things he said seemed powerful, effective and binding, and his comment about me put me in my place. Perhaps I was a "dead man." Spiritually dead, like in the book of Jude, one of those people who are "twice dead" and "for whom the nether gloom of darkness has been reserved forever." Stewart had given the older brothers one last chance and we were not responding to this opportunity to be restored to the faith. Was the displeasure I felt from Stewart really God's displeasure toward me? Was it God's righteous wrath toward me, a hardened rebel, one who had "thumbed his nose at Jesus?" (This is what Stewart accused the older brothers of.) Was I spiritually dead and on my way to hell? It was hard to tell. God was showing me things and waking me up to the reality of life in COBU through these adverse conditions. But I was tired, wiped out, and I certainly did not have a good relationship with God.)

The sisters who managed the books in church office noticed that a certain amount of money was going to 810 every week and receipts for the same amount were not coming back. (The older brothers who Stewart accused of having an iron grip on the church's business had a couple good habits that these ones didn't have. They didn't steal money and they got receipts for everything to account for how the money was spent. But some of these new brothers, now freed from our iron grip and given the chance to move up in the church businesses and hierarchy had different ideas about how to run things.)

I first became aware that there was a problem one morning when Paul and I were sanding the wood floors in a restaurant. Robert and Claude came into the restaurant. This was unusual, because they never came to job sites. They wanted to know if we had any receipts we hadn't handed in to the office yet and if we did, they wanted to have them. They were asking everyone for receipts for the next few days and they looked worried.

I didn't know that the church had decided to shut 810 down on an emergency basis, because I wasn't there when the message came from the church office to the older brothers who lived there. They told the older brothers that the building was being shut down and that they should get together late in the evening to decide which of the new disciples could go with them to live in the Lamb House, which was COBU's other residence in the city. The rest of the new people could just leave. Paul, Peter, a new disciple helper and I had a job that night, so we weren't there for the meltdown.

I had no idea what was about to take place. Around 10 p.m., before this message had been sent over to 810, Paul pulled the van around front and we loaded the wood floor machines and supplies that were kept on the first floor there. I walked out with the last crate and got in the van. Just as we were pulling away, I had an unusual feeling and I said something to Paul without really thinking about what I was saying and having no apparent reason for saying it. I said, "I feel as if I'm being saved out of a great disaster that's about to happen, like being rescued from a shipwreck." Something catastrophic was about to happen and as we drove away, I felt as if I had been taken away from this event. It was just something I said. The night went on and I didn't think of it again.

We drove to a nearby suburb to our night job in restaurant with an Irish theme, called the Rose Cafe. After the last customers left, we began sanding the floors and cleaning the carpets. These restaurant jobs were good to be on at night. I was able to get away from the place I was staying in. No one was there except for me and my older brother friends, the small cell of brothers I worked with. They allowed me some freedom of expression and personal space without running the usual party lines on me, just so long as I watched it, which meant as long as I didn't say anything negative about Brother Stewart. We worked. We brewed coffee and ate crackers and any snack foods we could get our hands on. We didn't help ourselves to steak, but we ate the peanuts at the bar and we had all the soda we could drink, but we never touched anything else at the bar except for the soda machine.

Day broke and it was time to go back. We went to a diner for breakfast and Paul called the office and that's when he found out about the scene that had gone down at 810 soon after we left. When Paul got off the phone, he told us that the place had been shut down and there had been a riot. Over the next days, I got more details.

Later I heard from a middle brother, Stuart R., who was there when it happened, that some pushing and shoving started and that when he tried to defend a brother named Milton, a big guy who went by the name of Keith X picked him up over his head and threw him into the corner "like he was a towel." The new brothers were angry and had scores to settle with some of the older brothers who were there and they had scores to settle with each other as well. Their racket was being shut down and they were being put out on the street. (Later, the new brothers were given an opportunity to come back and to explain why they wanted to still live with us and some did, but these were the innocent ones and not those who had been running the racket.)

Paul (an older brother from Jamaica) was on the upper floor and some of the ones who weren't violent warned him that others were coming up to get him and that they had a gun. Rather than face whatever was coming his way, Paul went out on to the ledge and climbed down to the street on a tall sign that was attached to the front of the building. Later I heard from some of the new brothers who were there that these ones had intended to kill Paul. Paul could have been shot or beaten up, or injured if he lost his grip as he went out the fourth-floor window. The new disciples began to fight among themselves and the older brothers were huddled together in one of the rooms on the top floor. Stuart said he saw Ron stand up and look out the window, down to the street below, as if to consider leaving through the window too, and then he rolled his eyes and sat back down.

There was a meeting shortly after and Stewart, using the sisters' committee and the live-out church members to talk to everyone, wanted to know what happened and why no one had ever spoken up about what had been going on there. (During the time the wrong behavior was going on at 810, surely someone knew about it, they wondered.) Various brothers talked. I felt I should be honest and I verified a story given by someone else that there might have been a gun and that Robert said he had a gun in the trunk of his car. They asked me why I never said anything. I was at a loss for words. How could I explain how I was not able to talk about any problems to the same pastor and to the same committees who had been trying to push me out the door and who had been using these new disciples on me as a method of punishment? When Stewart came to the building, he wouldn't speak to the older brothers. He only talked to the new people, who were now being labeled as thugs, asking them how they were doing with their Christian training and if they were getting on the older brothers. I had no words to explain this to them. I just stood there. I didn't know what to say. I felt neither good nor bad, nor did I feel responsible or guilty for not having told anyone. Who was I supposed to tell this to and how was I supposed to go about it? They went on to question others and forgot about me. I was not really one of those they wanted to call to account. They wanted to grill the so-called celebrities.

Another thing happening at this time was that the church's new labor force was not doing very well. The new disciples went out with their push carts. Some came back at the end of the day and handed in the money from their sales. Others disappeared and spent the money on drugs and later, having nowhere else to go, they came back and tried to say they had been robbed. The pushcart business was not successful and it was obvious that the older brothers were still needed to make money for the church. I was with a group of brothers who were sent to "live on a homeless basis" in the Christian Brothers Cleaning business office at West 51st Street in Manhattan. We slept on the floor and had to be out in our working groups from early morning to late evening, looking for new customers and closing jobs. Ten of us were crowded into this small office. We slept on the floor after the sisters who worked there left around 11 p.m. and we got up in morning before they came back. The office was cluttered with desks, filing cabinets and now, crates and duffel bags filled with our belongings. It was obvious to me that Stewart had failed to get rid of the older brothers and that he still needed us to make money for the church. Through some graciously worded offer, he was now giving us the opportunity to prove ourselves by looking for customers day and night, on a sudden-death basis, which meant that if we didn't close enough jobs, we would be thrown out. After a month or so of this, we were able to move back to Woodruff Avenue again, where I had been before this whole adventure started.

Around this time, I began to have dreams that my father died. I want to mention this because of how family visits were handled in COBU, especially funerals and weddings. One day, I walked into my room at Woodruff and as I did, I heard the words, "a death in the family" pronounced in my mind. I thought of my father. And I tried to ignore it. Soon after, I had a dream where I saw a coffin. I didn't see who was in the coffin, but I thought about my father again. I called my father that day, almost expecting no one to pick up the phone. But he did, so I knew he was alive and I didn't think much of it afterward. A week or so later, I had a dream where I walked into the back yard of the house I grew up in. It was cloudy and there was somber light. My brother Mark was sitting on a garden bench, looking sad. I asked him, "Why do you look so sad?" He said to me, "Didn't you hear? Dad had a heart attack and he died." I said, "Yes, I know, I had a dream about it. The dream said, 'Dad is dead.'" After this, there was a movie-like sequence in the dream that showed things that I remembered about my father. There was low evening light and he was driving home from work and pulling his car into the driveway. A song I remembered from those years was playing, almost as if it were a soundtrack for the dream. Not long after, I was in the city, going door to door looking for carpet cleaning work and I heard this song being played in a store and I remembered the dream. That Saturday, in a morning meeting in the Woodruff basement, a brother came down to tell me that my sister-in-law called and that she said that it was important to call her back. As I walked up the stairs to the phone, I was thinking, "I'm not ready for this." When I got her on the phone, she said, "It's about your father. He had a heart attack and…. he didn't make it."

We were not supposed to go to weddings or funerals, unless we were going to "take a stand for Christ." Stewart said that in both of these events, the people of the world played a lot of games and if we didn't take a stand, we would end up taking part in these games. For weddings, Stewart said that these marriages were not based on Christ and that really, the couples were just fornicating. For funerals, he said that the living sat around and told lies about the deceased, such as how good the person had been and that they were in heaven now, when really, that person went to hell. If we didn't take a stand and tell those present that "unless you repent, you shall also likewise perish," then we were taking part in their deceit and games. Because of that, I decided not to go to my father's funeral, because I couldn't see talking to my family that way. Probably not so much coming from sparing them from this hellfire and brimstone as much as saving myself from the pressure of having to act that way.

All of this was ultimately set in the context of separation from our families. Stewart said that when Jesus said, "let the dead bury their own dead," he meant that those in the world were spiritually dead and to let them deal with their own funerals. But Jesus never preached against going to funerals. When Jesus said to let the dead bury their own dead, he was talking to a man he called to follow him and the man replied, "Let me bury my father first and then I'll follow you." This man wanted to wait until his father died, so he could inherit his estate, and then he wanted follow Jesus later. But Jesus told the man to follow him now, not later. I didn't have a thorough grounding in the Bible, even though I was in a church called The Church of Bible Understanding. I only knew what Stewart told us. It seemed plausible. Jesus said, "let the dead bury their own dead." I talked to brother Jim G. about it and he told me that he couldn't tell me whether to go or not to go, but that I should study the Bible for myself to see what it said about it and then make my own decision.

A few years earlier, I had decided not to go to my youngest brother's wedding, for much the same reasons. When I mentioned in passing to a brother named Rocky that my brother was getting married today and that I wasn't going to his wedding, he looked dumbstruck and said to me, "What? You're not going?" His normal, human reaction gave me a moment of clarity and I left immediately, hoping to get there in time and I did. I didn't speak up about how it was wrong for them to get married and I even enjoyed being with my family. No one in my family spoke to me about being in the cult. Some of us drove to my Uncle's house after the wedding and stayed for the night and then they dropped me off at the station where I took a train back to the cult. My mother smiled at me as I boarded the train. The only question she asked me as I was boarding the train was why the train had no locomotive and I explained to her that it was an electric train and that the motors were on the axles, and she smiled, as if to say, that's my son, he knows so much. People have asked me why my family didn't try to talk to me about leaving the cult. I really can't answer that question. It was more like, well, he looks okay. Maybe they didn't understand the true nature of a cult. Maybe they thought I would leave it in a while and that questioning it would only drive me further into it. I was going to leave the cult seven years later, and I was going to have to go through a lot more abuse in order to get to that place.

Chapter Thirteen

The Kingdom of the Cults

I always found some way to take a break from the intense work schedule of the church business. When I could, I walked back from a job site instead of getting a ride with everyone else. When I worked until late the night before, I made sure I was not in too much of a hurry to get back to work the following afternoon. And when I had to drive to pick up supplies, I stopped for a few minutes at a street overlooking the Hudson River, which was appropriately named Freedom Place, to collect my thoughts. There were some brothers in COBU who thought it was wrong to have any private life, especially now that Stewart was driving that we had to "break up our hideouts" and "no going off into our separate rooms." We were never supposed to be alone. We were supposed to be living and working in teams all the time and preaching Stewart's words and slogans to one another all the time. I had to be careful to keep my breaks hidden and to work loopholes in the schedule to get this free time.

One of the escapes I took were visits to the library, where I read books on foreign languages and other things I was interested in. I still had a desire to "evangelize" (although we didn't call it that). In my early years in the church, I thought we were going to "preach the gospel to the ends of the earth," as Jesus said to do, and speaking languages like French might help. Learning a language was acceptable in COBU in those years, but in my last years there, we were under extreme pressure to "break up our lives in this world" and to "kill everything in ourselves." It became hard to pursue any interests other than the agenda of the cult. This message came from every angle and it became an ever-tightening trap that was hard to escape from, even in my inmost thoughts.

(This extreme self-denial was based on Stewart's twisted interpretation of Colossians 3:5, in which the Apostle Paul exhorts believers to "put to death what is earthly in you." Stewart's intention was for us to give up our needs and interests and to devote our entire lives to pursuing his interests. He presented these arguments so convincingly and so constantly that it seemed like this was what the Bible said to do. If you didn't study and think on your own and come to your own independent conclusions, these teachings, combined with a communal life where everyone else was living like this and the exhausting treadmill of jobs, meetings and lack of sleep, became an overpowering force that was nearly impossible to fight against. It created a powerful undertow that dragged you beneath the waters and swept you away in its raging current. There were those who gave up and went along with the flow, but there were also those who enforced this way of life on the others by reporting them for any and all infractions.)

One day, while in a library on West 23rd Street, I noticed several books about cults on the shelves. I was curious, but I thought I shouldn't read them. On some level, I realized that if I read any books about cults, it would open up a can of worms and there would be no going back once I started reading them.

I was already open to the idea that I was in a cult, because at one time, Stewart himself used to accuse us of having a "cult" among us. According to Stewart, there were a number of church members who were suppressing the truth through their unfaithfulness to Christ and as a result, there was a subgroup among us, which he labeled "the cult." It was never clear who was in the cult and who wasn't. It was more like some mysterious force among us. None of us believed we were in the cult, but we did think a lot of the others were. If anyone looked dull, wiped out, dirty and tired, and acted uptight and unreal, I usually figured they were in the cult, not realizing that they looked that way from working long hours in the church businesses, sleep deprivation, the dirty and crowded living conditions, a less than ideal diet and the general frustration that resulted from living according to this way of life. When I was a middle brother, I thought that all the older brothers and sisters were in the cult and that I was in danger of being drawn into it and that my only way of escape was by being "fully there for Jesus, every second," or I too would become like them.

Sometimes it was embarrassing when the cult was mentioned. In my first year in the church, we met a young man who was interested in the church and who began to visit the fellowship house in Jersey City. I wanted to explain more about the church and our work in Haiti, so I showed him a postcard a brother sent us from our orphanage there. The brother had written few lines about the work in the orphanage and added that he was coming back to the States soon and that when he did, he "hoped to escape the cult." My new friend read the card and I saw him tense up and grow silent. He asked me what was meant by the cult. I told him, "That just means a group of people among us who are acting unreal." But this didn't help much. He never came back again. A house full of people living communally who carried Bibles already looked like a cult to him. He was interested, but cautious, and this alerted him that there might be a problem. And besides, we *were* a cult.

What that brother who sent the card meant to say was that he felt free at the orphanage, but once back in New York, it would be a different story. His words reflected his anxiety about the pressure Stewart put on us. We had to prove we weren't taking part in the cult. The brother knew that although he was doing well now, he was not likely to stand up to the usual treatment during his visit. He would be accused of being unfaithful to Jesus and would have to make a commitment to start over. It would be a letdown and he would return to Haiti discouraged. Or maybe he wouldn't be allowed to go back.

One time, I ran into Becky, a sister from the church, in an office building. As we stepped into an elevator with some other people, she turned to me and said, "We have to escape the cult!" I stared forward silently and hoped no one thought I knew her.

So, that day in the library, I became curious. I opened one of the books and looked at the table of contents. One of the chapters was, "The Cult as a Social System." I was hooked. I put the book back and didn't read it, because my usual fears kicked in. But it was only a matter of time before I came back to read about the social system of life inside a cult.

I had always observed our COBU "society" and thought about the way we acted toward one another. Our pecking order, the way church members snapped into line when a message came down from on high from Stewart and about how conversations among us were peppered with the phrase, **"Stewart said."** And about how Jim G. was second in command in the church and that whatever he said could not be contradicted, even when it seemed to me that he was acting wrongly, because he was a deputy leader under the authority of Stewart.

So, I read about the social system within cults and thought, "Yes, this is true." The book wasn't about COBU, but I could identify with the social dynamics it described. What was significant was that by reading this book, I was now willing to face that I was in a cult, or that I could be in one. I was willing to study and to do something about it. It was part of my trajectory toward leaving, helping to place me on the path toward getting out. The books I began to read made things clearer to me. I was already aware of some of these things, but I hadn't been able to fully understand them or to reason through them on my own.

Next, I read a book by the controversial deprogrammer, Ted Patrick. He was often hired by the parents of teenagers who had joined cults. He made drastic interventions which included kidnapping and isolating cult members and bombarding them with information about the cult they were in. The examples in the book were about groups that I clearly understood to be cults, such as the Unification Church. (One of the characteristics of cult members is that they believe that all the other cults are cults, but they don't think they're in a cult.) Maybe Ted Patrick's methods were drastic and sometimes questionable, but as I read the reasons he gave for his actions, I liked him and understood some of his viewpoints. (Though I wouldn't suggest that anyone arrange to have this done to someone in a cult.)

Once, a brother named Steve told me about how his parents hired a deprogrammer who abducted him during a home visit. If his parents had known what was going to happen, they probably wouldn't have hired him. Steve said the deprogrammer was a Jewish guy by the name of Svi who locked him up in a room and tied him to a bed. One of Svi's methods was to tell Steve, "So you believe in God? I'm going to jump off this dresser and land on your chest. Now, why don't you pray to God when I'm in mid air and ask him to stop me. Do you believe that God is going to do that for you?"

When hiring a deprogrammer, it might be good to check first if he's only going to try to deprogram your kid from being in the cult and if he can show him that he doesn't need to be in the cult to serve God, instead of trying to deprogram your kid from believing in God. These are not one and the same thing. Steve later escaped through a window and hid under a car. He heard Svi say, "Steve, I know you're under there, now come out." So he came out. Svi later returned Steve to his parents and Steve later returned to the cult.

Another day, we were sanding the wood floors in a psychologist's apartment in Manhattan. There were bookshelves all around her living room, so we put plastic drop cloths over the shelves to protect the books from sawdust. I could see the books through the plastic as I sanded the floor. So, during breaks in the work, I pulled back the drop cloths and looked at any books I was interested in. One of the books was called *Total Institutions*. (I had already begun to consider COBU to be an institution in the sense of it being a bureaucratic system with fixed rules where the rank and file members were regimented like cogs in a machine, and that if any discipline or trouble came my way, it was because I stepped out of my place on the assembly line and that any correction was not for my own good, but only to put me back in my place so the machine would function smoothly again. I also considered COBU to be like the Russian communist society that Alexander Solzhenitsyn wrote about in his books *The Gulag Archipelago* and *A Day in the Life of Ivan Denisovich*. So, I was already prepared for the ideas I found in this book about total institutions.)

As I was glancing through the book *Total Institutions*, the words seemed to jump off the page. I was reading an explanation of my own daily life, in terms I had not understood it in before. Now, I don't want to make this a list of the books I read and a review of their contents. I just want to say that these were not merely intellectual exercises. I could identify deeply with the concepts in these books. Another important book I read at the time was *Escape from Utopia* by William Olin. I identified with his experience and how he escaped from the cult he was in. It was like reading a book about myself. These and other books helped me to understand what was going on in the cult, especially during our all day long pressure cooker meetings with Stewart. The concepts in these books were now the lens through which I was able to see and understand what was going on. They provided a buffer zone, insulating me from the intense heat and pressure of these meetings. Much of the heat and pressure came from believing it was all true. If I could detach myself from it and believe a different explanation than the one Stewart gave us about the processes taking place at the meetings, then I had some room to begin thinking about it, instead of only reacting in the moment and running from the bolts of wrath and the flames of hellfire being shot at me. I could begin to ask myself, "But what if it is not God who is doing this to me?"

I would not have been able to escape COBU by only reading the Bible and comparing it to Stewart's teachings. (Although this helped.) Because religious doctrine was not the only thing holding me there. Few people join cults because of doctrine and few people leave cults because of doctrine. They usually leave when cult life wears them down or when they become aware of the vast difference between the way the cult leader tells his followers to live (usually lives of abstinence and self-denial) as compared to the way the cult leader lives (a wealthy, hedonistic lifestyle, surrounded with a harem of female followers). Stewart did his best to hide his wealth and to make it appear that the entourage of female companions was there to help his wife (they were called the "Gayle Helpers," not the "Stewart Helpers"), but still, the difference between the way Stewart told us to live and the way he lived was glaringly obvious. Stewart claimed that the things he had were a reward for his faithfulness to Christ and that our lack of these things was the result of our unfaithfulness to Christ. This claim was convincing at times (it was the official party line we had to pay lip service to), but this claim could not completely explain away the difference in lifestyles, except to the most ardent and sold-out believer.

The book about total institutions made frequent reference to a book called *Asylums* by Ervin Goffman. (Including Goffman's observation that a total institution is any organization that controls every aspect of its inmates' lives, and that it is often a live-in situation. This was like a book about my life and about where I was living.) Not long afterward, I found Goffman's book at a street bookseller's table. A basic point in this book is that most people have three spheres in their lives, in which work, family and leisure activities take place in separate locations. In a total institution, all of these activities are carried out under one roof, and what happens in one area affects the other areas. In COBU terms, this meant that if I disagreed with my pastor, I could find myself summarily fired from my job and put out of my place of residence. This would be nearly impossible to do to someone who was not living in a total institution. People in whose lives these areas are separated can disagree with their pastor in church on Sunday and can still go home for the night and show up for work on Monday, because their pastor is not their landlord and employer. Living in a total institution put me in a position of being extremely controlled.

Now it was more clear to me how Stewart held absolute power over me and why I caved in immediately the year before when I spoke up to Stewart at a meeting. During this meeting, Stewart was asking us, "What's wrong here? What's the real story?" This always meant we were going to talk about what was wrong with the older brothers and what we were going to do about it. But instead of offering an opinion about what was wrong with the older brothers, I told Stewart that he was what was wrong here. I said I believed that his repentance at the Grace Meeting had been genuine, but that I thought he had gone back to the way he was before and that in fact, he was even worse than he was before. I said, "You need to talk to other pastors, because you're alone and you need to get your views checked."

There was a sudden uproar as the brothers stood up from their seats and began to shout me down. A brother asked me, "Are you saying that Stewart is your problem?" I said, "No, but I am saying that he's causing some problems." Stewart asked everyone, "What's he really doing?" A brother said, "He's very subtle. I don't trust what he's up to." Stewart prompted the brothers by asking, "Would you say he's attacking?" A brother answered, "He's attacking the gospel!" Another said, "He's not just attacking you, he's attacking all of us!" Stewart agreed and added, "Not only that, he's attacking the very *basis* of the truth." Stewart continued to prompt the brothers until they were demanding to have me put off the church property immediately. Someone shouted, "I say he goes right now!" And others shouted in agreement. Now faced with the sudden threat of having no job and nowhere to live tomorrow, within seconds I was saying I was wrong and pleading for forgiveness. I was able to beg to not be immediately carried off the property and I was put on a three-day sudden death, meaning that if I didn't mend my ways, I would be thrown out. (The three-day sudden death was given only to the most violent of the new disciples.)

Until that moment, I had expected that Stewart would consider what I had to say, because he portrayed himself as a man of truth who always considered the truth, no matter what the source. I soon found out just how wrong I was and that truthspeaking only flowed from the top downward. I naively believed that the worse that could happen is that Stewart would say he didn't agree - especially now that he said he had changed and because, when he told us he had been teaching in error all those years, he asked us, "Why didn't anyone ever tell me?"

I got a long message from Stewart later in the week which he dictated over the phone and which Joe read to me off a couple of file cards. Stewart's message was that I was refusing to accept reality and that as a result, I was losing my mind and it was starting to show in my behavior. He counseled me to stop fighting against reality and he offered me a chance to join in something greater than myself. Stewart often said that brothers were losing their minds or that they were mindless. He said we hoped to lose our minds so we wouldn't have to serve truth or because we couldn't bear the thought that we were going to hell. He said we were retreating into insanity as a way of escape from truths that were just too horrible to face. Stewart considered that anything less than one hundred percent agreement with his views meant that we weren't accepting the truth about God, life, ourselves and all of reality.

Over time, as I studied these books, I began to face that I needed to leave COBU. Sometimes I tried to bury all of it and to just forget about it, because it was just too much to deal with and because I got threatened when I talked about it. But no matter how deeply I buried it, these thoughts and realizations about life in the cult came seeping back up to the surface, like buried toxic waste. Sometimes I spoke up about what was wrong about life in the cult. This was because I hoped that by speaking up about it, I could change things, and then I wouldn't have to leave. Stewart always told us that Jesus commanded us to "speak the truth." I was to learn in no uncertain terms that speaking up about anything wasn't going to help and that my brothers and sisters would be more than happy to separate themselves from me and to quarantine me - that is, to keep me away from the new people so I couldn't to talk to them, because I was "poisoning" them with my ideas. Ideas like how we should fully inform the new people, up front, about what life in COBU was like and what they were getting into, instead of letting it dawn upon them over time, while we sold them an idealized (and untruthful) version of what life there was about and what we were really using them for.

Chapter Fourteen

My last Year in COBU

Around this time there was very intensive training new of disciples at Woodruff Avenue. The older brothers worked all day and then stayed up till late at night with the new disciples in long meetings whose purpose was mostly to vote and judge everybody's performance, to make confessions and recommitments about wrong behavior, with a little bit of Bible study thrown in. Sometimes we went on for hours dealing with transgressors. Stewart wanted to do some housecleaning and to remove any of the older brothers who were not pulling their weight or seen as not contributing to the work. These brothers were separated from everyone and sent to live in the Red Hook warehouse. They were now banished and had to try to prove themselves worthy enough to move back to Woodruff to rejoin the work. (One of Stewart's tactics was to create a punishment category and a favored category and then to use the tension between the in and out groups to drive people to work harder. Those in the punishment category worked harder to prove themselves worthy to be allowed back in and those in the favored category worked harder in order not to be put in the punishment category. These categories had different names over the years, but this method was always in use during the years I was in COBU.)

I was one of those who were selected to be in this punishment category. I felt put down, but I was also glad to move out of Woodruff once more. This punishment had some side benefits. (As long as I didn't look too happy about it, which would have been the fastest way to be sent back to Woodruff.) I didn't have to stay up anymore until two in the morning every night. I could get some sleep instead. And there were no crowds of new disciples who were so tightly packed into the building that it was like being in the subway at rush hour. The few new disciples who were labeled as troublemakers and sent over from Woodruff to live with us in Red Hook were usually not so bad. They were only acting up because of the way they were being treated at Woodruff, and we cut them a break at Red Hook. I was now living in a one-story Civil War era warehouse that had some character to it. It was on a cobble stone street in a quiet corner of the Red Hook section of Brooklyn, about five blocks away from the really bad areas. Unlike Woodruff Avenue, the street was quiet at night and I could sit in the door of the warehouse and enjoy the night air.

We were supposed to be working to "prove ourselves" to go back to Woodruff Avenue, but whenever I heard news of what was going on over there, I was glad I wasn't there anymore. The irony, which the brothers at Woodruff never seemed to understand, was that every week we had a meeting with Stewart and the result was always the same. Stewart accused the brothers at Woodruff of "cheating," which meant that in spite of their hard work, they were "still trying to have it both ways." He accused them of secretly desiring to keep their lives in this world, instead of putting their lives in this world to death. And despite their hard work and selfless service, Stewart always accused them of being lazy and proud. The brothers had to agree with and confess to the charges and recommit themselves to trying harder next week. I wondered what the point was of going back to Woodruff to burn out like that, only to be told that what I had done all week was "games and cheating." And any shame of being in an out-group in the church was not enough to motivate me to wipe away the social stigma of living at Red Hook by proving myself worthy to move back to Woodruff.

And if at one time, I used to worry that no sister would be interested in marrying me if I wasn't "united and in fellowship with all of my brothers," that fear was long gone. I understood by now that I would never be able to have a relationship or get married in COBU. I knew this from experience and from having a greater understanding from my reading about why cults forbid or at least tamper with the marriage relationship and why total institutions suppress the formation of households. Relationships were competing and alternate loyalties to our leader and his program. We were all were expected to look directly to Stewart and only to Stewart and not to have alternate loyalties, relationships or interests of any kind. We were pawns in an income producing machine and we were housed inexpensively in a group living situation to keep costs down. Allowing relationships, marriages and families would disrupt this system. Stewart also wanted the choicest of the sisters to live with him and he may also have wanted to discourage marriages because any sisters who knew anything about him that should forever remain a secret might tell their husbands about it if they were in an intimate relationship with one of the brothers in the church.

(An example of a group that tampered with, but allowed the marriage relationship is the Unification Church. Members of that group had to wait three years to be assigned a spouse and then had to live apart for three more years until they could get married. This ensured six years of hard work out of marriage-minded members of that group. After 1979, the waiting period for marriage in COBU became indefinite.)

And I understood by now that COBU relied on a workforce without ties to a location or a family, which could be deployed to any location in the church at a moment's notice. We only needed to throw a few changes of clothing in duffel bag and go. As a workforce, we had no legitimate reasons or conflicting interests, such as wanting family time, as a reason to turn down the long hours of work in the church's businesses.

We were all supposed to sleep in an open common area in the Red Hook warehouse, on the floor or on the shelves that were used to store rolls of carpet. Paul had already built a small shack inside the warehouse for the wood floor equipment, which he kept padlocked so theft-minded new disciples couldn't walk off with power tools to sell on the street. And when we moved to the warehouse, Paul set up the shack so he and I could use the shelves as bunks to sleep on at night. When some of the older brothers protested about our "wood floor shack hideout" and said they were going to tell Stewart about it, Paul reminded them that he was letting them keep their power tools in there for safekeeping. That always worked. He threatened to tear the shack down if we couldn't live in it and then they could worry about their power tools on their own. When Peter, the other member of our wood floor team, was sent to Red Hook, he slept in the common area first, but he begged to move into the closet with us because he was terrified of the rats that infested the common area. Paul built an extension on the shack for Peter and now the three of us slept in there at night.

This arrangement lasted for over a year. The fire department discovered that we turned the warehouse into a residence and ordered us out, so we spent a couple of nights at the office in Manhattan, but we moved back in under Stewart's directive to make sure it didn't look like anyone lived there. So every morning when we left, we stacked supplies and machinery on the bunks to make it look like the shack was used for storage only. But later, Stewart ordered us to move to the church's office on West 46th

Street in Manhattan, which was over a garage, so we could be in fellowship with our brothers and so we could be there for the morning meetings on time. There was a large area in the back that was used to store carpet and to have meetings and once again, I was sleeping on the floor under a desk at night.

Chapter 15

Leaving COBU

When I began to speak up about my new understanding of how the COBU system worked, certain things started to happen. In a closed community like COBU, all dissent was quickly noticed. Even minor differences in behavior stood out against the backdrop of total conformity like a smudge on a white wall. And all dissent was swiftly dealt with. I was quarantined and marked as a troublemaker. Some of the brothers and sisters said I shouldn't even be allowed to speak. I wrote and passed out a statement about what was wrong with the church and why I wanted to leave it. This paper also included a call to action where I asked others to write papers and to discuss what was wrong with the church and how we could change it. No one wanted to read the paper, except for Paul, who agreed to let me read it aloud to him as he was driving. He told me there was one point in the paper he agreed with, but when I asked him what it was, he wouldn't tell me. On the following Sunday, a sister said to me in a sarcastic tone from across the meeting room, "I heard about your letter of love." (The brothers and sisters sat on separate sides of the room. There was an aisle down the center of the room as a line of demarcation between the brothers and the sisters.)

Whenever I began talking about my new understanding of life in COBU, others quickly moved in to shut me down. Some took a more conciliatory approach and directed me to look to Christ's sacrifice on the cross instead, because they said this was the real issue. But nobody wanted to discuss these ideas with me. There was only one place for a person like me, and that was out. Years after I left, I found out that some of the brothers who slammed me the hardest also used to talk in private about what was wrong with Stewart and the church. But in public, I was met with a unified wall of denial and opposition. I spoke up to Stewart at a meeting one last time and instead of being threatened with being put out, I was ignored. After I deflected a few questions from brothers who stood up to refute me, the entire room grew silent and I sat back down.

If I wanted to stay in the church, the only route available to me was confessing that I was wrong, and that meant renouncing all of my objections, never speaking of them again and towing the party line from then on, or else no one would believe that I had truly repented. I would have to say that I made up all these ideas as a clever deception in order not to have to be obedient to Jesus. I would have to admit that "my flesh is always looking a way to deny the truth and to try to have it both ways." These kinds of phrases, which were a standard part of the dialog for all COBU members, could be jumbled in any order, as long you said enough of them and they were not your real thoughts on the matter. I could have said, "My flesh is trying to have it both ways, so I can indulge my pride and keep fighting against Jesus." Or I could have turned it around and said, "I'm fighting against Jesus, so I can indulge my pride and so my flesh can have it both ways."

I would then be expected to say what I planned to do about it, now that I had admitted to my rebellion. So, I would need to add, "But I commit myself to putting my pride and arrogance and my flesh to death." If I wanted to emphasize how much I meant this and to show that it was "not just a speech," I could throw in extra words like *fully* and *urgently*. "But I *fully* commit myself to *urgently* putting my pride and arrogance to death and *urgently* putting my flesh to death." And this would be acceptable as some kind of renunciation of my rebellion. (Some brothers and sisters were skilled at stringing long chains of these cult phrases together, for example, "I see how, all the more, starting from now on, I really need to urgently face the real truth, every second, about my own sin and to urgently put my flesh to death or else I'm really just cheating and trying to have it both ways. I'm in big trouble and I'm not going to get away with it and neither are you.")

But what if I had something I really wanted to talk about? But through years of being bullied and badgered by Stewart, we learned that this how he wanted us to talk and that these were the only words he wanted to hear from us. This is how the brothers and sisters talked to each other and it was what anyone was directed back to saying if they tried to speak in normal language. If a brother said he was not happy about life in COBU or talked about any problems he was having, a brother would say to him, "Isn't your real problem pride?" Or, "Isn't the real issue that your flesh is fighting to have it both ways?" The brother was then expected to confess that he had been into pride. He could only speak and be spoken to according to these terms, because everything else was "not the real issue." People who study mind control techniques (commonly known as "brainwashing") call these phrases "thought-terminating clichés." These phrases are used to shut down dialog, to put an end to dissent or to justify false reasoning.

Robert Jay Lifton, one of the foremost researchers on mind control, said "The language of the totalist environment is characterized by the thought-terminating cliché. The most far-reaching and complex of human problems are compressed into brief, highly reductive, definitive-sounding phrases, easily memorized and easily expressed. These become the start and finish of any ideological analysis." - Robert Jay Lifton, *Thought Reform and the Psychology of Totalism. A Study of "Brainwashing" in China* (The University of North Carolina Press, 1989) 429.

The use of the thought-terminating cliché is one of the defining characteristics of the Church of Bible Understanding and we achieved a level of mastery in it that defies all comparison. This is one of many features that make COBU one of the worse mind control cults of all time, because of how deeply members have internalized this way of thinking and speaking. All dialog between church members is dominated by this kind of language and they express everything according to it.

In George Orwell's novel, *Nineteen Eighty-Four*, the State designed a language called Newspeak which was designed to limit thought. All words were removed from the language that didn't reinforce the total dominance of the State. And all words for concepts (such as *rights* and *freedom*) that could be used to argue against the leader, who was called Big Brother, were eliminated.

"The purpose of Newspeak was not only to provide a medium of expression for the worldview and mental habits proper to the devotees of IngSoc [*English Socialism*], but to make all other modes of thought impossible...[it] was designed not to extend but to diminish the range of thought, and this purpose was indirectly assisted by cutting the choice of words down to a minimum... In Newspeak it was seldom possible to follow a heretical thought further than the perception that it was heretical: beyond that point the necessary words were nonexistent." -George Orwell, *Nineteen Eighty-Four*, from the chapter, *The Principles of Newspeak*.

One of the most used thought-terminating clichés in COBU at the time I left was "Your own sin is your basic problem, not circumstances or the other bad guys." Generally speaking, this is a true statement. According to the Judeo-Christian worldview, the greatest challenge facing human beings is their own sinful nature, which has the power to separate them from God for eternity, which is a greater problem than any other circumstance in life. Other religions and philosophies speak of mastering oneself or overcoming one's lower nature as the greatest challenge, which are related ideas. But Stewart didn't introduce this as a great religious truth we could benefit from, but only as a way to control us. The phrase "Your own sin is your basic problem, not circumstances or the other bad guys" was used to shut people down who complained about living conditions or long hours (circumstances) or how they were being treated by others or by Stewart (the other bad guys). No one dared to speak these words to Brother Stewart when he was telling us what bad guys we were or when he was not pleased with circumstances in the church. But in COBU, there was always a ready-made answer for everything, including this. We believed that Stewart did have his sin problem conquered. He had taken the log out of his own eye first and now he was able to see clearly to remove the log from our eye. And having turned (to be fully obedient to Jesus), Stewart was able to "strengthen the brethren." There were so many levels to this reasoning **that most gave up and didn't try to fight against it.**

One day, Dave and Chris, who were former members of the church, came to the church office to talk to the brothers and sisters. I fought and argued with them, as did everyone else. Later I called them to apologize about the way I had acted toward them. I told them that I was with a new brother at the time and that I felt compelled to protect this brother from them, even though I agreed with everything they were saying about Stewart and the church.

This is not the first time I ever encountered ex-members who I agreed with. A couple of years before this, we ran into a former COBU brother named Tod who could not be kept quiet about what was wrong with the church. After first joining in the usual fray that took place during these encounters with ex-members, I realized that I agreed with everything that Tod was saying. I didn't see how I could keep telling him that he was wrong and that he had to come back to the church, as the brothers I was with were doing. I walked away and sat the rest of the brawl out. What was different now was that I was ready to leave COBU and that I no longer considered those who left to be the enemy. They were just people who understood what I now understood, only they had come to realize it long before I did.

I began visiting Dave and Chris at their apartment when I was able to get away. They told me I could move in with them if I wanted to. I deliberated for a couple of weeks after getting this offer. Despite how bad it was in COBU and what was pretty obvious to me by now, I still needed closure and I needed to finish a few things. And leaving was a big step. I was going to leave with nothing, except some clothes and books, and a few hundred dollars in the bank. But I considered what would happen if I continued to stay and how much harder it would be to leave as the years went on. If it was like this for me when I was 36, what would it be like when I was 45 or 50 and had less strength and even fewer options? At least now there was still time to start my life over. I didn't know Dave and Chris very well, but this was my one offer and if I wanted to leave, this was the way to do it. A few weeks before this, I had written a letter to David Wilkerson of Times Square Church describing what it was like to live in the Church of Bible Understanding and I invited him to talk to Stewart. I still hoped that if Stewart talked to other pastors, he might get some help. David Wilkerson didn't call Stewart, but he knew that Dave and Chris had been in COBU and he told them, "Help that brother in any way you can."

I finished my last wood floor job in COBU, a night job in a restaurant. When I came back to the church office, I decided to borrow a church van from the parking lot across the street to take my things over to Dave and Chris's apartment, and then bring the van back and leave. Then I discovered I didn't have my driver's license in my wallet. And the parking lot attendant told me the church was behind in paying the lot fees. He said he wasn't going to let me have a van unless I gave him forty dollars and I didn't have that much money. I stood there deliberating what to do. Maybe it was a sign that God was telling me I shouldn't leave? But everything I had experienced over the last few years pointed to that I should get out. I even believed that God was showing me to get out. I thought, if I don't leave now, I'll never leave, so I ran back up the office stairs to get my duffel bag and then I caught a cab at the corner and showed up at Chris and Dave's apartment. I was still in the COBU business mode from years of habit, so when the cab driver asked me what I did for a living, I told him I sanded wood floors. He told me he wanted the floors sanded in his new house, so I gave him a Christian Brothers business card and told him to call us. I was finding new customers for the cult, even as I was fleeing from it.

Later that evening, I went to help Paul put polyurethane on the wood floors in an apartment. As I was working, I said to him, "I left the church." He asked me, "Then what are you doing here?" I told him I was there because I knew he needed help finishing the job. When we finished, we walked to the corner and Paul went down the stairs at the entrance to the subway. Paul barely said good bye, even though we had lived and worked together nearly every day for the last three years. I kept walking in the warm night air to Dave and Chris's apartment, which was not far away. I was now free and out of COBU after being in it for fourteen years. Physically speaking, leaving was easy. I just changed residences. At the same time, leaving was not an easy process and it took years for me make the decision to leave, even after beginning to seriously consider that I was in a cult.

Chapter 16

Free at Last

When I walked out of COBU at the end of August 1993, I entered a new world. I was now living on the Upper West Side of Manhattan with Chris, Dave and Dennis, who had left the church several years before. It was only a taxi ride from the church's office on West 46th Street to get there once I decided to leave, but the journey to get to that point had taken many years. And it had not been a straight line, because I often thought of leaving, but didn't.

Being with ex-members of COBU who understood what I had been through made it easier for me to transition from life in the cult to the outside world. I started going to Times Square Church in Manhattan, where there were about 50 ex-members who attended regularly. They said the same things about Stewart Traill and the church that I had thought about while I was still in the cult. Dennis explained why he believed there was no marriage in COBU. He said it was for economic reasons and as a way to have a small army of single and unattached people available to work day and night. I couldn't believe that someone else had come to the same conclusions and was speaking about it in the same way I had been thinking about it. Until then, I had only my own observations and it was often hard to believe my own thoughts. There were also the many books I read, but there weren't any books written about the Church of Bible Understanding in which someone explained everything in a systematic way. There was nothing that specifically explained how and why Stewart Traill did the things he did or why the brothers and sisters acted the way they did, and to tell me what to do about it. So, it had been up to me, my observations and any help in understanding I got from books about cults, institutions and totalist environments, plus a study of Christian history and particularly the history of Christianity in America, where I learned that there have been hundreds of small groups like ours.

There were some brief references to the Church of Bible Understanding and the Forever Family (COBU's original name) in books published before 1979. These references were outdated and there was no information in print about COBU from 1979 onward. It was easy then for me to believe that this information about COBU was true, but that it described the conditions in COBU before Stewart said he found grace and repented, and that now things had changed for the better. Toward the end of my stay there, a more current description of COBU was published in a chapter of the book *Churches that Abuse* (Ronald M. Enroth, Zondervan, 1992), but I thought it was an angry ex-member's story. I was trained to believe that ex-members were backsliders who invented malicious lies about the church to divert attention from what they were really doing, which was that they were rejecting the truth and looking for an easier way than the hard way to heaven that Jesus talked about. Jesus said that the road to destruction was wide and easy and that many people were on it and that the road to life was hard and narrow and that there weren't many people on that road. But for us, this narrow road meant being in COBU and following Stewart's teachings. All other ways were false. Even though I was coming to believe different things about those who left COBU (such as how thousands of people can't all be wrong), these deeply implanted fears and beliefs had the nasty habit of kicking in and keeping their hold on my mind whenever I did any serious thinking about the church and my place in it and when I was considering leaving it. It was hard to think objectively about it.

I often spent entire Sundays in Times Square Church, going to the morning, afternoon and evening services and going out to eat with ex-members and making acquaintances with people who had not been in COBU. Spending long hours in church was normal for me and after years of being in long meetings in COBU, being in church all day on Sunday (and attending evening services on Tuesdays and Thursdays) was nothing compared to that. Eventually I cut down the all-day Sunday routine, realizing that I was not being less spiritual if I only went to one of those services. Also, it was information overload to go to three services on a Sunday, all of which were scripted and crafted to lead to an altar call at the end of the sermon. As time went on, I became annoyed as I sensed the cues about mid-sermon that were leading up to the big altar call, when it seemed that half the church came running forward to the front of the stage to receive whatever it was that had been preached about in the sermon. I sensed a kind of manipulation going on, although it was nothing compared to what I had been subjected to during my years in COBU. But still, I sensed it and I didn't like it.

What was good about Times Square Church was that there was a committee of pastors who were accountable to one another and who were not lone rangers like Stewart Traill was. These were men of integrity, such as Bob Phillips and others. And it was good to hear David Wilkerson preach. I trusted him, and pastoral trust, post-COBU was a major issue. I read Wilkerson's book, *The Cross and the Switchblade*, many years before and I had tremendous respect for him because of what he had done. And here I was, actually seeing him, yet it was not like celebrity worship.

And besides, I wrote David Wilkerson when I was still in COBU, and he told Chris and Dave to reach out to me and to do anything they could do to help me. If he hadn't prompted those brothers to help, they might not have offered me a place to stay and my journey to leaving COBU could have taken longer and it's possible that I might still be there. (I say this because sometimes in earlier years when I was considering leaving - though I had no concrete plan, just a wish to leave - Stewart often started some hopeful-sounding program that made me hope again and reapply myself to cult life and put all thought of leaving aside. Stewart was notorious for sensing unspoken discontent among us and when necessary, holding out some carrot on a stick, some motivational program, while being a little friendlier toward us (that is, laying off the abuse for a while and telling us hopeful things about ourselves, like how we just needed to hope in God's love for us).

The leading pastors of Times Square Church knew about Stewart Traill and COBU. They had even tried to contact him. (He wouldn't talk to them, but that didn't surprise me.) When Pastor Bob Phillips found out that a large number of people who were ex-members of our church were at Times Square Church, he wanted to know more about them, so he held a series of meetings with ex-COBU members to hear their thoughts and to offer advice. (After I left, I listened to the tapes of these meetings.) Bob Phillips said that we had been living under a system that didn't include the grace of God. He also said that there had been good things in COBU, but that it had been mixed with deadly poison, like good food laced with rat poison. I remember listening to these tapes through a pair of headphones when a group of us went to a state park. I lay there on a rock by the lake, looking up at the trees and the sky, and it was good to hear a well-balanced explanation of what life had been like without the love and grace of God and what we could do now to be close to God.

It got progressively worse for those in COBU after I left. I heard that Stewart was compelling the brothers and sisters to say, "I volunteer for the lake of fire," meaning that, by their actions, this is what they were really saying with their lives. The closest I had seen to this before was when Stewart spent a good part of one meeting trying to make Joe say that he was a child of the devil. Joe said that he wasn't a child of the devil, but Stewart kept saying, "But what do your life and your actions say?" which meant that by his lifelong record of cheating and unfaithfulness to Christ (as Stewart alleged), Joe was not only proving what his eternal destiny was, but also his true origin. This comes close to inducing a Christian to blaspheme, in my opinion. Joe kept responding to Stewart's line of attack by saying, "I know that my actions don't look good and it could appear to be that way, but I can't say I'm a child of the devil." And Joe said this as many times as Stewart asked him the question. Stewart finally gave up on Joe for the time being. I heard that there were many volunteers for "the lake of fire club." The twisted rationale that church members believed, and which was always the script, was that only by admitting to their desperate eternal state, their depravity, sinfulness and lifelong record of rebellion, was there any hope for them. If they denied their wretched condition, they would be lost and damned to hell for sure, because they were believing that they were okay and that therefore, they didn't really need Jesus to save them. Stewart's utter degradation of church members continued and worsened as the years went on.

No one came looking for me when I left COBU. This was unique, because usually when anyone left, we made an effort to find them and to convince them to come back. This was also a form of belief reinforcement for us, because we put on a hard sell to discontented members about how our way was the best way to live. I used to keep a list of family addresses I copied from the covers of letters written to brothers and sisters in COBU, so if they left, I had the names and addresses of parents and other family members to try to find them with. We often went after people who left and sometimes we convinced them to come back. Part of this convincing was getting them to give up their doubts and complaints about life in COBU and about Stewart Traill.

A brother named Bernie left COBU and came to stay with us at Chris and Dave's apartment, then he went back to the cult. He came and went several times until he finally left for good. Cult counselors call this a revolving door exit. It can take some cult members several attempts until they finally leave. COBU is known for being a cult with one of the highest return rates because of how deeply its members have internalized the teachings of COBU. They also have the feeling that they need to be deeply committed to Christ and not to go to church only on Sunday, like all those lukewarm Christians in the "world." Many former members can't get on with their lives, or think that their lives are a failure because they're not in COBU anymore, instead of thinking that their lives were negatively affected because of being in COBU and that this is the source of their problems. From time to time, I saw these ones come back and try to re-enter COBU life. For many, the shock was too great because the living conditions had become so terrible and the way of life was militant. One brother returned, but by the next day, he was saying, "I can't live like this!" while being surrounded by a cluster of brothers who were telling him that the living conditions were not the real issue and that he needed to be in COBU to escape going to hell. The brother was gone that afternoon.

After I left, a brother who left 15 years ago and who had a successful cabinet business was so troubled about not being in COBU that his friends and clients told him that he needed to make up his mind either to go back or to forget about it, because it was ruining his life. He came back, moved into the church's residence at

Woodruff Avenue in Brooklyn and what he experienced during the next few weeks was enough to cure him of COBU forever. He thought it would be like the early days, when brothers and sisters sang together and went witnessing for Jesus. This returning brother was shocked by the courtroom-style meetings in which brothers were interrogated about their faults and made desperate fever-pitched recommitment speeches while being shouted at by all the others, the cramped and dirty living conditions, the mindless shouting back and forth of slogans, the monitoring of one another and reporting to Stewart. All of this existed to some degree even in the early years of the church, but by this time it had become a totalitarian society.

Kevin and Chuck sometimes called for Bernie when he was staying at Dave and Chris's apartment to try to get him to come back to the church. Dave asked Kevin, "So how come you never call for Jim LaRue to try to get him to come back?" Not that Dave thought I should go back, but the reason was obvious. I spoke up about what was wrong with COBU (and what should be changed about it) and about what was wrong with COBU's leader. It was dangerous to allow these ideas to be openly discussed and considered, because if I were allowed to get away with it, others might start speaking up too. I wasn't just complaining about the long work hours and living conditions, where my complaining could just be written off as whining. I had well-reasoned ideas and I was willing to talk about them, and because of that, no one wanted me back. A person like me had to be eliminated and forgotten. Now, if I said I left because I was a worthless sinner and that I was no good, they would have encouraged me to come back. And if along with that, I said I had a few misgivings and complaints about life in the church, they would have said that these complains were not the real issue and that the real issue was my sin and rebellion. People who agreed to these terms were always welcomed back into the cult. The only way anyone could come back was on their knees, repenting and laying aside all of their complaints.

(I always thought there was a secret underground reservoir of disagreement among COBU members about our way of life and that if Stewart ever acknowledged that there was any legitimacy to our concerns, it would be like a dam breaking and there would be no stopping it. Allowing this would have had diminished Stewart's control over us, since the typical controls and restraints of a totalitarian society - such as the suppression of dissent, controlling the language we used and a system of monitoring everybody - were needed to keep the cult running the way he wanted it to. When Stewart said he was repenting from his former behavior, he also admitted to having caused us some problems. This helped me to hang on a while longer and to reapply myself to cult life, because I believed he was going to change for the better.)

A few days after I left, I had to go to the church office because I had left my driver's license with the sister who kept the books because she needed to make a copy of it. I went to the office with Dave and Dennis. The COBU brothers who were there, including Joe (the one who Stewart tried to make confess to being a child of the devil), launched an all-out verbally violent attack on Dave and Dennis. It was like a bar room brawl in an old western movie, but without the punching and throwing things, because COBU brothers weren't physically violent and they didn't swear either. The brothers were merciless and inhuman in their attacks on Dave and Dennis as I stood by, completely ignored. A similar scenario was repeated in April of the next year when I needed my tax return information (from working at the church's business) and I had to almost beg for it on the phone. I hinted at legal action if they didn't give it to me.

It's a COBU custom to give a nasty workover to anyone trying to get their tax information or their belongings after they've left. Church members think they're taking part in a person's sin just to let them have these things without putting up some kind of fight. Also, they might try to withhold it to get them to come to the church so they can talk to them about returning. When I finally went to get my W-2 which stated my earnings for working in the church's business and a document that said I had "donated" all of my income to the Church of Bible Understanding in return for room and board, Joe summarily handed me an envelope at the door and then shut the door in my face. Dave stayed downstairs in the car, not wishing for any of the usual abuse.

EPILOGUE

Some more things you may want to know about The Church of Bible Understanding:

COBU is a world-separating cult, not a world-embracing cult. (Cults and also mainstream religious groups can be one or the other, or somewhere in between.) Members of a world-embracing cult move freely among the people in the world, engaging in and using all the things of this life freely. Family visits, relationships and marriage are encouraged. A world-embracing cult is also less likely to be a live-in, communal group. In world-separating cults, there is a strict separation between who is in the group and who is outside of the group and there is a rigid divide between life in the cult and life in the outside world. In legitimate world-separating religious groups, this separation is an attempt to remain pure from the temptations and distractions of the world. Monasteries are a good example of this. There are many verses in the Bible about keeping oneself separate from the world. These groups interpret this separation more or less literally, but not always in a way which is harmful to the members of those groups.

In COBU, the separation is not so much about purity, as it is for control, and insofar as possible, to make Stewart Traill's viewpoints the lens or filter through which church members see all of reality and to remove all other influences from their lives. When I became aware of this, I began striving to find other viewpoints about life and Christianity because I didn't want Stewart to be my sole arbiter of reality. Other people who weren't bought into Stewart's worldview were a source of conflicting information, so these people were excluded from our lives as much as possible. We only talked to people outside our group for two reasons: recruiting new members or because they were our customers. I only became aware of how separated I was from the rest of the world when I began reading about cults and learned that cult members only talk to people outside of their cult when recruiting or fundraising. Until I read those lines, I had never considered this before. Although we didn't call it recruiting and fundraising (we called it "witnessing" and "working in the business"), I realized it was true nonetheless. When I considered my isolation from the rest of the world according to this way of looking at it, I realized just how locked up and lonely I was.

Stewart's effort to isolate us began when we were younger. Stewart often spoke to us about leaving our families in order to follow Jesus. He quoted Jesus, who said, "He who loves father or mother more than me is not worthy of me," and "a man's enemies will be the members of his own household." (These quotations are from the Gospel of Matthew, chapter 10.) Really, Jesus's first words here were about priorities. Most Christians believe that people who put God first can love their families better. Jesus's warning about family members being enemies was about future times of persecution when some Christians' own family members would hand them over to the authorities. Stewart took these sayings out of context and turned them into an absolute, meaning that if we wanted to visit our families or to have more than only occasional contact with them that we were loving our families more than Jesus. When brothers and sisters said they wanted to visit home to be a better influence on the lives of younger siblings or to care for a sick family member, Stewart said that the best example this brother or sister could give their family was to be faithful to Jesus, right here in COBU. Stewart said our families would act as our enemies and try to discourage us from following Christ. Now, this doesn't mean that everyone agreed to this. Many left the church because of these strict rules, but this also filtered out those who were not completely obedient to Stewart's teachings, leaving an ever-tightening net of influence on those who remained, who were surrounded only with others who believed in this way of life.

Ex-members are even more strongly avoided because they no longer believe in Stewart's worldview and they understand how the COBU system works and are not as easy to fool as those who are not as familiar with the group. It is interesting to note however that when a current COBU member is leaving, usually the first person they contact is an ex-member, because ex-members are among the few who can relate to their experience and understand what they're going through.

Another issue is what COBU defines as "the world." COBU draws the line tighter than the Bible does, by considering the world to be "all that is not of COBU." At the same time, if greed, sexual immorality and lies are of the world and not a part of the true church, then the world is alive, well and living undercover in COBU. The Bible describes false religion as "holding the form of religion, but denying the power of it." COBU holds the form of a strict and pure religion but denies the transformational power of religion to its followers, placing them instead under a yoke of oppression and bondage. Yet many of the rank and file members honestly want to serve God. There are sincere people in COBU and there are those who are in leadership positions who carry out Stewart's orders on the others and who are poised to take command when Stewart dies.

It would be hard to sift through Stewart Traill's life to find some redeeming qualities that would speak well for him. Although Stewart held the top position in the Church of Bible Understanding, it seems that most church members got some benefit from the church not because of him, but in spite of him. There is a proverb in

Latin that says, *Senatores boni viri, senatus mala bestia*, which means "the senators are good men, but the senate is an evil beast." I think that for the most part, people in COBU were and are good people. Most of us joined when we were teenagers or in our early twenties at a time when COBU was a bunch of happy and enthusiastic kids who had no idea of what it, and our lives, would become. But the organization itself, or the way the organization was led and what aims it has been used for are at best utterly selfish and perhaps evil. The Church of Bible Understanding was, and still is, Stewart's income producing machine and a captive audience and stage upon which Stewart can play the role of the great and all-knowing Bible teacher.

The current state of COBU revolves around their architectural antique business called Olde Good Things. (But, as this story has shown, our lives in COBU were centered in working in the church's businesses in times past as well.) There is little or no drive to preach the gospel anymore. New workers are hired and don't have to be members of the church. Stewart and a few church members, mostly women, live in a mansion in Florida. Stewart Traill, the man who preached against the evils of having a life in this world and about working hard and suffering for Jesus, is living a rather good and comfortable life in Florida.

www.ingramcontent.com/pod-product-compliance
Lightning Source LLC
Chambersburg PA
CBHW071455040426
42444CB00008B/1352